D1272272

DATE DUE

PLACE-NAMES
OF
THE WORLD

PLACE-NAMES
OF
THE WORLD

ADRIAN ROOM

DAVID & CHARLES : NEWTON ABBOT

Set in 11 on 13pt Aldine Bembo
and printed in Great Britain
by Latimer Trend & Company Ltd Plymouth
for David & Charles (Holdings) Limited
South Devon House Newton Abbot Devon

CONTENTS

INTRODUCTION

The aim of this book is to give the derivations of over one thousand of the world's place-names. Nearly all the countries of the world and the majority of their capitals are included; a wide range of major natural geographical features (oceans, seas, rivers, lakes, mountains, islands, capes, deserts and the like); all American states and their capitals and all Soviet republics and their capitals; a large number of political and administrative divisions of countries (provinces, territories and so forth), some of which are strictly speaking historical but still widely used, such as the provinces of France; many towns and cities important because of their economic standing or historical associations; a selection of tourist regions and resorts; the chief regions of Antarctica.

As the emphasis of the book is on place-names of the world, and as there already exist a large number of works dealing with English place-names, I have included very few British names, with the exception of those of the constituent countries of the British Isles, the chief islands and island groups around the British Isles, and the three main Channel Islands.

The prime concern of the book is to give the origin of the names and not to deal with the places themselves. Any information of a geographical or historical nature given in the entry for a particular place is included to help elucidate the origin of the name. Put another way, the book is a toponymical rather than an etymological dictionary. Toponymy—place-name study—is, although a relatively new science, one that involves not merely the linguist but equally the geographer and the historian. The name of Dresden, for example, tells the linguist that the derivation is from a Slavonic word meaning 'forest'; the geographer will expect the city to be surrounded by a forest, as indeed it is; and the historian will be interested in the fact that at some stage in the past a Slavonic people was inhabiting what is now German territory. To the toponymist, however, and to the general student of place-names, the name will reflect all three aspects, and from its derivation he can learn that here is a city which was once inhabited by a Slavonic race and which was, and probably still is, close to or surrounded by a forest. In short, a place-name frequently gives a clue, or a whole set of clues, telling us its background and as often as not revealing an unexpected or perhaps unrealised aspect of its past.

This particular example illustrates an important if obvious fact: that a place-name is not a random thing. It is a name given, by a person or persons, even if in a form in which it is not known today, or in a language which no longer exists, to a particular place for a particular reason. What that reason was depends on a number of factors, but chiefly on the historical dating of the naming, the stage of cultural development of the namer or namers, and the social, political, religious or patriotic attitudes or motives of the namer or namers. At an early stage in the development of civilisation, for example, geographical names were given which simply indicated the nature or appearance of the place named, such as the Rocky Mountains or the Red Sea. At a more advanced level, many places were named after their owner, whether a whole tribe, as in the case of France, or an individual, as with the Weddell Sea. Yet another category of names is those that are virtually dedications—to a person, perhaps, to a historic incident, or even to another place of the same name—as is the case with, respectively, Vancouver, Réunion and Venezuela.

Broadly speaking, the simpler a name is, in whatever language, the older the place is likely to be. Thus the Yellow Sea, Madrid, the Volga and the Alps are all ancient names referring to the physical properties of the places—the silt washed down the river, the wood with which the town was originally built, the colour of the river and the rocks on the mountains. On the other hand, many ancient names reflect the names of the tribes or peoples who once lived there, as we have seen in the case of Dresden, and as is also the case with, for example, Bonn, also in Germany, but probably with a name of Celtic origin, and even Russia, with a name that is very likely of Swedish origin (though this is still disputed, not least, understandably enough, by the Russians themselves).

This one factor alone, that tribes were constantly migrating from one part of the world to another, only to intermingle with other tribes or to die out altogether, frequently complicates the toponymist's already complex task of determining the true origin of a name. His work is also made no easier by the fact that languages, like their native speakers, were similarly transferred and transformed and similarly became extinct, with the result that a place-name as we know it today may be quite different in form and pronunciation from its original version, and may very well have changed a number of times as new people, speaking different languages, successively inhabited it. Just one simple example of this is Istanbul, which until quite recently was Constantinople and originally Byzantium —not to mention that at one stage it was also New Rome and, to the Slavs, Tsargrad.

There is, however, a historical era, beginning roughly in the Middle Ages, when—although there are always exceptions—it is possible to see a definite pattern emerge in the bestowing of place-names. Many names, for example, with the element 'bridge' or 'ford' (in any language) are of medieval origin, since it was frequently at a particular bridge or ford over a river that a town or settlement would grow up. This was the case with Bruges in Belgium, Pontoise in France, Osnabrück in Germany, Alcantara (from the Arabic) in Spain, Zamość in Poland and, of course, Oxford and Cambridge in England.

A little later, in the 15th and 16th centuries, a whole succession of religious names—mostly saints' names—were given by Spanish and Portuguese missionaries, settlers and explorers. Frequently a place would be named after the saint on whose feast-day it was sighted or founded (this was particularly true of the great Italian-born but Spanish-serving explorer Columbus), thus incidentally helping the historian to determine not only the year but the very day when a place was discovered or settled. Such religious names are especially abundant in Central and South America and the West Indies.

In the following three centuries it was the turn of the French, English and Dutch colonisers to sprinkle their names in newly settled or discovered countries, notably in North America (French and English), Africa (French, English and Dutch) and Australia (English and Dutch). The place-names of North America, and in particular Canada, present a special problem as in many cases they are direct translations of American-Indian names—into French or English, or even into French and then into English—which frequently were originally those of tribes or tribal leaders rather than their territories (on the basis that a particular tribe or Indian chief would own and occupy a particular territory), and of which the original form has rarely been accurately recorded. Many of the place-names of the United States, however, still survive in their Indian form—just over half of America's states have Indian names—but have meanings that, because of corrupted or incorrectly preserved forms, are open to dispute. These

9

names of the 17th, 18th and 19th centuries were not for the most part religious in origin, but, where not translations from native names, were those of important national rulers and leaders and their families, as illustrated by the Orange Free State, Adelaide and the still frequent and ubiquitous Victoria.

Finally, in the 20th century, and providing one more labour for the already Herculean task of the place-name researcher, there has come a kind of full circle in which, as countries that were once colonies achieve independence, still further names appear, many of them paradoxically but understandably ancient (in the native language), such as Ghana and Sri Lanka. This is especially in evidence, of course, in Africa, where a country on achieving independence will not only assume a new name but will re-name most of its towns and cities and, in fact, any place that has a 'colonial' name. In a different context, but for similar reasons, one of the countries that in the present century has had what must arguably be the greatest 'place-name turnover' in the world is the Soviet Union, where since the 1917 Revolution hundreds of places, from the largest of cities to the smallest of streets, have acquired new names—and sometimes with not just one change of name but several successively (see *Pushkin*, for example).

Every place-name is, therefore, at any given moment in time, a sign of its times.

It is perhaps to be expected that European place-names are better researched than any others. The sociologist may also be interested to discover that they are the most prosaic. Compare, for example, Germany's Cologne (colony), France's Provence (province), Italy's Apennines (peaks) and England's Northampton (town in the north by a meadow) with North America's fresh and colourful Medicine Hat, Alabama and Baton Rouge. Yet some of the best-known European places have names that to this day, and after exhaustive research, have not yielded one conclusive meaning. Even world-famous capitals such as London, Berlin and Moscow have had so many derivations ascribed to them that it would be a major undertaking—and quite impossible in the present book—to quote them all. In a number of cases, too, many places have acquired not merely an uncertain etymology but a completely false one. A common example of this is when a legend or mythical character comes to be associated with a place in an attempt to explain an unknown name—a 'folk etymology', in fact—and then subsequently the name is popularly explained as deriving from the legend or mythological figure, instead of vice versa. A familiar instance of this is Rome, supposedly founded by its first king, Romulus, and named after him. But Romulus, like his twin brother Remus, belongs to Roman mythology (he was the son of Mars, the god of war) and not to reality. The same is true of many figures of classical mythology, so that the links between Europa, loved by Zeus, Atlas, who supported the sky, and Athene, patroness of arts and crafts and goddess of wisdom, and Europe, the Atlantic Ocean and Athens are, alas, only links in name. Some of these legends and mythical links are, however, either so well known or so original, both in and beyond Europe, that in a few cases I have felt it valid or interesting to quote them (see, for example, *Warsaw*, *Berne* and *Ararat*).

If well-known place-names cause such difficulty and confusion—and 'folk etymology' is only one example of this—it is not surprising that comparatively few of the world's place-names have been really accurately and satisfactorily explained. And even if one toponymist reaches a (to him) conclusive explanation of a name, it is very likely that another, equally 'reliable' authority will give a completely different derivation. (This is to say nothing of the unintentional or purely careless mistakes that creep in when one authority is basing his material on that of another.) It is for this reason that the entries in the present book contain with what must seem bewildering frequency the terms 'probably', 'possibly' and 'perhaps' which, I should explain, are not given arbitrarily, but are used to give the following shades of meaning:

'probably' means that the information given, although not finally established as correct, is, as far as can be told from the facts available, likely to be the most reliable, and is generally accepted;
'possibly' means that the information given is based on incomplete research or conflicting data, but nevertheless is acceptable as a serious attempt at explanation until further facts are available;
'perhaps' means that the information given is inconclusive, likely to seem inconsistent when compared to other known facts, and yet worthy of serious consideration in its own right (ie it is not ruled out altogether as impossible).

When working with such seemingly unstable and even unreliable material, I am all too aware that in a book of this kind, which must itself rely heavily on other sources, there is a very real possibility that inaccuracies will have been passed on, as indeed I have found to be the case in the authorities I have consulted. I have not, of course, knowingly or deliberately included inaccurate information, and have in fact gone to considerable pains to ensure, by means of checking and cross-checking in a number of works, that the derivations given are as reliable as possible, given the data available. In certain cases, however, where different authorities have been at variance with one another over the derivation of a name, or where there has been obviously conflicting evidence, I have used my judgement to give what seems to be the most likely explanation, always aiming to give in controversial instances 'probably' rather than 'possibly' and 'possibly' rather than 'perhaps'. There are, of course, names whose origin cannot even now be guessed at, and I have not hesitated to include these—if only to show that little or nothing *is* known about certain place-names and to illustrate the fact that place-name study is not only a complex and at times frustrating subject but also an infant science which, although now rapidly developing, is not yet really much out of its cradle.

In spite of an increasing tendency for place-names in present-day atlases, encyclopedias and reference works to be given in their native version or spelling, I have given in almost every case the accepted English variant of a name, so that Zaragoza, Köln, Vlissingen and Livorno are dealt with under Saragossa, Cologne, Flushing and Leghorn. But where a place is known by two equally acceptable names—even if one is now historically inappropriate—I have given both, often with a cross-reference, as with Madagascar and the Malagasy Republic, Siam and Thailand, Mount Godwin-Austen and K2, Canton and Kwangchow. Similarly, although the majority of place-names dealt with are the modern ones, I have in a few cases included information on the former name or names of a place, either under the modern heading, or in one or two instances, where it seemed historically justifiable, separately: thus a reference to Tsaritsyn appears under the heading for Volgograd, but St Petersburg and Petrograd are dealt with separately from Leningrad, under their own headings. There are also cases where I have thought it interesting or useful to include the native name of a place, or that used by a neighbouring country for it, under its accepted English name, so that under Everest there is an explanation of its Tibetan name of Chomolungma, and under Lake Lucerne a reference to its German name of Vierwaldstätter See.

As explained, the book is highly selective, and for this reason I have not included self-explanatory names such as the Rocky Mountains, the Indian Ocean, the English Channel or Northern Territory, Australia. Here again there are a few exceptions: where the 'obvious' name has a background or a meaning that is perhaps not quite so obvious, as is the case, for example, with the North Sea or the Blue Mountains in Australia, I have included it.

Each name is followed by a brief geographical 'pointer', so that it can be located and so that confusion is avoided between similar names (such as Dominica and the Dominican Republic, Montpelier and Montpellier, Granada and Grenada). The locations as given are deliberately general, and compass bearings, in particular, are approximate, and are given to 'two significant letters' (ie south-east not east-south-east). The descriptions are brief but should be adequate to determine what the place is and where it is. Other names mentioned in descriptions which have their own entries are cross-referenced.

In conclusion, I should like to think that this book, in its admittedly modest scope, may prove of interest not only to professional toponymists but to all who are attracted to the study of place-names and who can appreciate the important part they play in revealing to us the historical, social and linguistic background of the many countries and cultures of the world.

LANGUAGE GUIDE

The following notes are designed to serve as a guide to some of the ancient languages mentioned in a number of the main entries in the book.

Amharic: the ancient language of Ethiopia (Abyssinia) dating back to the 11th century BC. It exists today as the modern state language of Ethiopia and is spoken by about 6 million people.

Carthaginian: the ancient language of North Africa (in the region with Carthage as its centre) spoken by emigrants from Palestine. It is one of the forerunners of modern Hebrew.

Celtic: the ancient language of the Celts, the people who originally inhabited southern Germany before 1000 BC and who later overran France, Spain, Portugal, northern Italy, the British Isles and Greece. It is represented today by the Gaelic languages of Ireland and Scotland, by Welsh and by Breton.

Etruscan: the ancient language of the Etruscans (Tuscans) who inhabited northern Italy (modern Tuscany) some time before 800 BC.

Gaulish: the ancient Celtic language of Gaul (modern France), which died out about AD 600 with the introduction of Latin.

Germanic: the ancient language of the Germans, a large group of tribes speaking a common Indoeuropean language who before 100 BC inhabited a territory in central Europe bounded by the lower Rhine, the Vistula, the Danube, and the Baltic and North Seas and southern Scandinavia. Germanic languages today are divided into: 1. East Germanic (Gothic, now extinct); 2. North Germanic or Scandinavian (Icelandic, Norwegian, Danish, Swedish); 3. West Germanic (German, Dutch, Friesian, English).

Gothic: the extinct Germanic language of the Goths, a people who settled on the shores of the Black Sea about AD 200. They disappeared as a nation in the 5th century AD.

Iberian: the ancient language of the Iberians, the pre-Celtic people who, about 1600 BC, inhabited the Spanish peninsula and south-west France.

Illyrian: the ancient language of the Illyrians, who, before 1800 BC, inhabited the coastal region on the Adriatic in what is now north-west Yugoslavia.

Indoeuropean: the ancient language of the people who about 3000 BC inhabited northern central Europe and western Asia. About 2000 BC their common language began to split into what is now one of the world's largest families of languages, including Hindustani, Sanskrit, Iranian, Slavonic, Germanic, Baltic, Latin, Romance (French, Italian, Spanish, Portuguese, Rumanian and others), Celtic, Greek, Albanian and Armenian.

Iranian: the ancient language of the Persians, whose chief modern descendants are Persian, Afghan and Balochi, spoken respectively in Iran (Persia), Afghanistan and Baluchistan by a total of about 30 million people.

Ligurian: the ancient language of the Ligurians, who, before 800 BC, inhabited the coast of the French and Italian rivieras. It survives as a north Italian dialect, spoken along the coast of the Ligurian Sea.

Old High German: a forerunner of modern German spoken in Germany between AD 700 and 1050. It was the language used by Benedictine monks for translating Latin church texts into the vernacular. ('High' because it was spoken chiefly in upper or southern Germany.)

Phoenician: a variant of Carthaginian spoken before 1600 BC by the Phoenicians, a people who inhabited what is now Lebanon but who travelled extensively and set up colonies in Cyprus, North Africa, Malta, Sicily and Spain.

Phrygian: the ancient language of the Phrygians, who inhabited Asia Minor (Anatolia) about 1200 BC.

Sanskrit: an ancient Indoeuropean language of India dating back to about 1500 BC. All the Indoaryan languages (Hindi, Urdu, Sinhalese, etc) are at least partially derived from it, and it has remained in use in India for sacred and literary purposes.

Scandinavian: the former common Germanic language of Scandinavia, now represented by Icelandic, Norwegian, Danish and Swedish.

Slavonic: the former common language of the Slavs, an Indoeuropean people who appear to have originated in the Carpathians, and who by the 7th century AD occupied the area lying between the Baltic, the Elbe, the Adriatic and the Black Sea. In the 16th century they were driven out of what is now East Germany. Their language is now divided into three groups: 1. eastern Slavonic (Russian, Ukrainian, Byelorussian); 2. southern Slavonic (Bulgarian, Macedonian, Serbo-Croat, Slovene); 3. western Slavonic (Czech, Slovak, Polish, Wendish).

ELEMENTS OF NON-ENGLISH PLACE-NAMES

The following list contains both separate words and parts of words. If the element usually begins a name, it is followed by a hyphen (as ober-); if it usually ends a name, it is preceded by a hyphen (as -leben). Capital letters, as for words and elements beginning a name and German nouns, are not given.

It is hoped that the list will help to explain at least part of the meaning of a number of place-names that are not given in the main part of this book, and that the language will serve as a guide to the geographical whereabouts of the place concerned or as a clue to the nationality of its namer.

-abad	Iranian	town
ain	Arabic	well, spring
al	Arabic	the
alt	German	old
alto	Italian, Spanish, Portuguese	high
am	German	on the
bach	German	stream
bad	German	mineral springs
bahia	Spanish, Portuguese	bay
bajo	Spanish	low
ban	Siamese	village
bas(se)	French	low
basso	Italian	low
baum	German	tree
beau	French	beautiful
bel-	Slavonic	white
bel(le)	French	beautiful
-berg	German	mountain
beth	Arabic	house
bianco	Italian	white
bir	Arabic	well
blanc	French	white
blanco	Spanish	white
blank	Germanic	white

bocca	Italian, Portuguese	mouth
boden	German	meadow
bolshoi	Russian	great
-bosch	Dutch	wood
bouche	French	mouth
-bourg	French	fortified town
-brod	Slavonic	ford
-brück	German	bridge
-brunn	German	spring, well
buena	Spanish	good
-burg	German	fortified town
-bus	Slavonic	dwelling place
-by	Scandinavian	town
byel-	Slavonic	white
cabo	Spanish, Portuguese	cape
campo	Italian, Spanish	field, plain
casa	Italian, Spanish, Portuguese	house
castelho	Portuguese	castle
castello	Italian	castle
castillo	Spanish	castle
château	French	castle
chow	Chinese	town of 2nd rank
cima	Italian	peak
città	Italian	town, city
ciudad	Spanish	town, city
col	French	pass, neck
colle	Italian	pass, neck
cordillera	Spanish	mountain range
costa	Italian, Spanish, Portuguese	coast
côte	French	coast; slope, hill
court	French	enclosure
croce	Italian	cross
croix	French	cross
cruz	Spanish	cross
dal	Norwegian, Swedish	valley
-dam	Dutch	dam, embankment
dar	Arabic	house, country
darya	Iranian	sea, river
de	French, Spanish	of
di	Italian	of
-dorf	German	village
-dorp	Dutch	village
el	Arabic	the

-ey	Scandinavian	island
-feld	German	field
fels	German	cliff
felsö	Hungarian	upper
fiume	Italian	river
fu	Chinese	town of 1st rank
-furt	German	ford
-garten	German	garden
-gau	German	province, district
gebel	Arabic	mountain
gora	Slavonic	mountain
-gorod	Slavonic	town
-grad	Slavonic	town
gran	Italian	great
grand(e)	French	great
grande	Spanish, Portuguese	great
gross	German	great
-hafen	German	port, harbour
hai	Chinese	sea, lake
haut(e)	French	high
heim	German	home, dwelling place, village
ho	Chinese	river
hof	German	settlement
holm	Scandinavian	island
horn	German	peak
hsien	Chinese	town of 3rd rank
-ia	Latin	territory (of)
île	French	island
ilha	Portuguese	island
-ingen	German	belonging to
isla	Spanish	island
isle	Old French	island
isola	Italian	island
-istan	Iranian	country
jebel	Arabic	mountain
kap	German	cape
kara	Turkish	black
ker	Breton	village
kiang	Chinese	river
king	Chinese	town
kirch	German	church
kop	Dutch	head, hill
krasno-	Russian	red, beautiful

kum	Turkish	sand
la	French, Spanish, Italian	the
lac	French	lake
lago	Italian, Spanish, Portuguese	lake
lang	German	long
las	Spanish	the
le	French	the
-leben	German	dwelling-place
es	French	the
los	Spanish	the
maly	Slavonic	little
-mark	Indoeuropean	boundary
matt	German	meadow
meer	German	sea
mer	French	sea
mont	French	mount(ain)
monte	Italian, Spanish	mount(ain)
most	Slavonic	bridge
-mund	German	mouth
nagy	Hungarian	great
nan	Chinese	south
negro	Spanish	black
nero	Italian	black
neu	German	new
neuf, neuve	French	new
nieder	German	lower
nizhny	Russian	lower
noir	French	black
nord	German, Dutch, Norwegian	north
nouveau, nouvelle	French	new
novi, nov(o)-	Slavonic	new
nowa, nowy	Polish	new
nueva, nuevo	Spanish	new
nuovo	Italian	new
ny	Danish, Swedish	new
ober-	German	upper, higher
-oe	Danish, Swedish	island
ostrov	Slavonic	island
oude	Dutch	old
para-	Indian (American)	river
peña	Spanish	rock
petit	French	little
pod-	Slavonic	under, below

-pol(is)	Greek	town
pont	French	bridge
ponte	Italian, Portuguese	bridge
pore (*see* pur)		
porto	Italian, Portuguese	port
pueblo	Spanish	village
puente	Spanish	bridge
puerto	Spanish	port
punta	Italian, Spanish	cape, headland
pur	Sanskrit	town
ras	Arabic	cape, headland
rio	Spanish, Portuguese	river
saki	Japanese	cape, mountain
san	Italian, Spanish	saint
santa, santo	Spanish	saint
são	Portuguese	saint
-see	German	sea, lake
selo	Russian	village
serra	Portuguese	mountain range
sierra	Spanish	mountain range
-sk(y)	Russian	belonging to
sous	French	under
sri	Sanskrit	holy
-stad	Swedish, Dutch	town
-stadt	German	town
-stan	Iranian	country
star	Slavonic	old
-statt	German	settlement, town
-stein	German	stone, castle
sur	French	on
-tal, -thal	German	valley
trans-	Latin	beyond, across
tre-	Breton	village
unter-	German	under, below
val	French, Italian	valley
vár	Hungarian	fort
veliky	Slavonic	great
verde	Spanish	green
viejo	Spanish	old
vieux	French	old
vila	Portuguese	town
villa	Spanish	town
ville	French	town

Elements of Non-English Place-Names

wad(i)	Arabic	river
-wald	German	wood
za-	Slavonic	beyond
-zee	Dutch	sea
zemlya	Russian	land

PLACE-NAMES
OF
THE WORLD

Names appearing in *italic* type
in this section of the book have
a separate entry in their own right

A   **Aachen** (city in west of West *Germany*, south-west of *Cologne*, near Belgian and Dutch frontiers)
From Old High German aha= 'water'; town was originally Roman settlement by mineral springs, with Latin name Aquae Grani = 'waters of Granus'. French name is *Aix-la-Chapelle*.

Aarhus (2nd largest city in *Denmark*, on east coast of *Jutland*)
From Danish aa = 'river' (+ 'r') + os = 'mouth'; city is at mouth of small River Molle which flows into *Kattegat*.

Abadan (seaport in south-west *Iran* near head of Persian Gulf)
From Iranian abad = 'populated place'.

Abruzzi (region in southern central *Italy*)
From Latin abruptus = 'abrupt, steep'; region is in highest and most rugged part of *Apennines*.

Abyssinia (alternative name for *Ethiopia*)
Portuguese name borrowed in 1520 from Arabic habash = 'black' (ie land of black-skinned people).

Accra (capital of *Ghana*, on Gulf of *Guinea*, West *Africa*)
Probably from African (Akan) ukran = 'black ant', name given to members of Nigerian tribes who came to settle in region in 16th century.

Addis Ababa (capital of *Ethiopia*, North-East *Africa*)
From Amharic addis = 'new' + abeba = 'flower'. Site for capital was chosen in 1887 by Emperor Menelek II.

Adelaide (capital of state of South *Australia*)
Named in honour of English queen Adelaide, wife of William IV, in whose reign city was founded (1836).

Adélie Land (*Antarctic* territory between *Wilkes Land* and King George V Land)
Named after wife of French explorer J. Dumont d'Urville, who discovered it in 1840.

Aden (territory in south-west *Arabia*, east of southern entrance to *Red Sea*)
From Arabic root = 'saddle'; territory consists of 2 volcanic peninsulas.
From 1967, part of South *Yemen*.

Admiralty Islands (in *Bismarck Archipelago*, north-east of *New Guinea*,
South *Pacific*)
Discovered by Dutch in 1616 who named them 'The Twenty-One
Islands' (there are in fact about 40). Renamed Admiralty Islands in 1767 in
honour of British Admiralty. (Not to be confused with *Amirante Islands*.)

Adriatic Sea (arm of *Mediterranean* between *Italy* and *Balkan* Peninsula)
Named after Roman city of Adria, probably in turn derived from Illyrian
adur = 'water, sea'. City was once (6th–5th centuries BC) a port but is now
14 miles (22km) inland.

Aegean Sea (arm of *Mediterranean* between *Greece* and *Turkey*)
Probably from Greek aiges = 'wave', though in legend name is connected
with Aegeus who drowned himself here on hearing, falsely, that his son
Theseus was dead.

Afghanistan (kingdom in central *Asia*)
Said to be from name of legendary forefather of all Afghans—Afghana +
Iranian stan = 'country'.

Africa (continent crossed by equator)
Probably from Arabic afira = 'to be dusty' (afar = 'dust'), word giving
name to Berber tribe of Afrigii or Afridi who BC inhabited region south
of Carthage. When Romans captured this city in 2nd century BC they
named the province they set up here Africa, after the tribe (territory of
province corresponded to modern *Tunisia*). Name then gradually spread
south to whole continent.

Aix (name of: 1. Aix-en-Provence, town in south *France*; 2. Aix-la-
Chapelle, French name for *Aachen*; 3. Aix-les-Bains, resort and spa in
Savoy, south-east *France*)
All derived from Latin aquae = 'waters' (ie mineral springs). Aix-en-
Provence was originally Aquae Sextiae, after Roman proconsul Sextius

who founded it in 123 BC; Aix-la-Chapelle is named after church here in which Emperor Charlemagne is buried (see also Aachen); Aix-les-Bains = 'waters of the baths'.

Ajaccio (capital of *Corsica*)
From Latin ad jacum = 'by the shore'; city is seaport on *Mediterranean*.

Akron (city in *Ohio*, USA)
From Greek akron = 'summit'; city is at top of divide between two rivers. Founded in 1825.

Alabama (southern state of USA)
From Indian (Cree) word adopted by first French settlers: perhaps alba-aya-mule = 'we clear a way through the wood', or alibamo = 'we stay here'. Name was that of tribe.

Åland Islands (at entrance to Gulf of *Bothnia*, *Finland*)
From Swedish å = 'water' + 'land'. Finnish name is Ahvenanmaa.

Alaska (state in extreme north-west of North *America*, belonging to USA)
From Aleutian A-la-as-ka (also rendered as Alaelisa, Alaxa) = 'mainland' (ie as distinct from *Aleutian Islands*). Originally belonged to *Russia* when it was known, in English, as Russian America. Sold to *America* in 1867 with assumption that native name = 'great land'.

Albania (republic in south-east *Europe* on *Adriatic Sea*)
Possibly from Arbenia or Arberia, medieval name of southern part of country, or from Illyrian olba = 'settlement'. Albanian name for country is Shqipëria, from Albanian shqipe = 'eagle'.

Albany (capital of *New York* state, USA)
Founded by Dutch in 1614 with name Fort Orange (see *Orange Free State*); renamed Albany in 1664 in honour of Duke of York, future English king James II, whose Scottish title was Duke of Albany (although there is no British place of this name).

Albert, Lake (in Central *Africa*, between *Zaire* and *Uganda*)
Discovered by English explorer Sir Samuel Baker in 1864 and named
after Prince Albert, husband of Queen Victoria. Native (Bantu) name is
Nyasa (see *Nyasaland*) Now Lake Hobutu Sese Seko.

Alberta (western province of *Canada*)
Territory named in 1882 by Scottish Marquis of Lorne, Governor General
of *Canada*, after his wife Princess Louise Caroline Alberta (also, no doubt,
with complimentary reference to Albert, Prince Consort, husband of
Queen Victoria). Constituted a province in 1905.

Albuquerque (city in *New Mexico*, USA)
Founded in 1706 and named after Viceroy of New Spain, Duke Albur-
querque. Omission of first 'r' may be result of confusion with better-
known Alfonso Albuquerque (1453–1515), Portuguese Viceroy of Portuguese Indies from 1508.

Alderney (most northerly of Channel Islands, close to west coast of
Normandy, France)
Roman name was possibly Riduna; later name was Adreni or Alrene;
probably from Old Norse word = 'island near the coast'.

Aleutian Islands (chain extending west of *Alaska*, USA)
Named after native inhabitants, Aleuts, with own name of uncertain
meaning. Not derived from Russian word lysy = 'bald'.

Alexandria (2nd largest city, and seaport, in *Egypt*, on *Mediterranean*)
Named after Alexander the Great, who founded it in 331 BC.

Algarve (province in south *Portugal*)
From Arabic Tarf-el-Garb = 'land in the west'; region was situated at
western edge of Arabian territory.

Algeciras (resort and seaport in province of *Cadiz*, *Andalusia*, southern
Spain)
From Arabic Jezir-al-chandra = 'the green island'; Arabs from African

desert landed here in 711 and were impressed by abundance of green plants.

Algeria (state in North *Africa*)
Named after its capital, *Algiers*.

Algiers (capital of *Algeria*)
From Arabic al-jezair = 'the islands'; city was built on 4 islands, joined to mainland in 1525.

Alicante (province of south-east *Spain* and its capital)
From Arabic name Alkant, in turn from Latin Lucentum = 'shining' (with reference to lighthouse).

Alice Springs (town in Northern Territory, *Australia*)
Named after wife of Sir Charles Todd, who established a base for a telegraph line here in 1872. Name frequently shortened to Alice.

Alma-Ata (capital of republic of *Kazakhstan*, USSR)
Founded in 1896 on site of Kazakh settlement of Almaty = 'apple, apple-tree'. City today is centre of fruit-growing region. Until 1921 name was Verny, Russian = 'true, reliable' (in sense of 'stronghold').

Alps (mountain system of south central *Europe*)
Probably from Celtic alp = 'rock, mountain', though perhaps connected with Latin alba = 'white'.

Alsace (historic territory in north-east *France*)
Of uncertain origin. Once thought to be connected with Indoeuropean aliso = 'alder'. No proof that name is derived from River Ill. Original meaning lost as early as 7th century, when was called Alsatia.

Altai Mountains (south *Siberia*, USSR)
Probably from Turkish alatau = 'speckled mountains' (ie covered with patchy vegetation and having snowy peaks). Or possibly from Turkish and Mongolian altan = 'gold'.

Amazon, River (longest river in world, in South *America*)
Probably from Indian (Tepiguarani) amazunu, amassunu = 'big wave',
with reference to famous bore (the pororoca) in lower reaches; name
was taken by Spanish explorers of 16th century to be derived from
Amazons, female warriors of Greek legend, since Indian women of the
Tepua tribe fought alongside the men (though Spaniards may have mis-
taken long-haired men for women).

America (great landmass of western hemisphere, divided into North
America, Central America and South America)
Discovered by Columbus in 1492, but named in 1507 after latinised
forename of Italian explorer Amerigo Vespucci, who in 1503 named
South America 'The New World'.

Amiens (city of north *France* on River *Somme*, north of *Paris*)
Roman name was Ambianum, after Celtic tribe Ambiani, with name
probably = 'water-dwellers' (from Sanskrit ambu = 'water'). Pre-Roman
name was Samarabriva = 'bridge over the Somme', from ancient name
of river—Samara— + Celtic briva = 'bridge'.

Amirante Islands (south-west of *Seychelles*, Indian Ocean)
Discovered in 1502 by Portuguese explorer Vasco da Gama and named
in his honour, as leader of the expedition, as Ilhas de Almirante = 'Admiral's islands'.

Amman (capital of *Jordan*)
From name of ancient Egyptian god Ammon, in sense of 'protected by
Ammon'.

Amritsar (city in *Punjab*, *India*)
From Sanskrit amrita saras = 'lake of immortality'; city was founded
around a sacred pool by Sikhs in 16th century.

Amsterdam (capital of *Netherlands*)
Named after River Amstel, on which city stands + 'dam' (ie 'dam on
River Amstel').

Anaheim (city south-east of *Los Angeles, California*, USA)
From name of nearby River Santa Ana + German heim = 'home'; town
was founded by German immigrants.

Anatolia (alternative name for Asia Minor, ie part of *Turkey* which lies in
Asia)
From Greek anatole = 'sunrise'; region is in eastern *Turkey*.

Anchorage (largest town in *Alaska*, USA, in south of state)
With simple sense of 'harbour, port'. Original name was Knik Anchorage,
but 1st word (probably Eskimo = 'fire') was dropped when town was
officially established about 1914.

Ancona (city and seaport in east central *Italy*, on *Adriatic*, capital of the
Marches)
Founded in 380 BC by Greeks from *Syracuse*. Name derives from Greek
ankon = 'elbow, angle', with reference to coastline on which city is
situated.

Andalusia (historic province in south *Spain*)
Named after Vandals, Germanic tribe who set up kingdom here in 5th
century AD. Initial 'v' from name Vandalusia was dropped by Arabs,
who conquered it in 8th century.

Andaman Islands (in north part of Indian Ocean, south-west of *Burma*)
Probably from Malay Pulo Handuman = 'islands of Handuman' (a native
god). Unlikely to be derived from handuman = 'monkey'.

Andes (mountain range in South *America*, running down west coast)
Possibly from Indian or Inca anta = 'copper' (found as a deposit in
mountains), or from Indian (Quechua) anti = 'east' (ie in relation to
Cusco, ancient capital of Incas).

Andorra (small state in *Pyrenees*)
Very old name, of unexplained origin. Perhaps connected with Basque
andurrial = 'heath'.

Andreanof Islands (west group of *Aleutian Islands*, in *Bering Sea*)
Named after Russian navigator Andrean Tolstykh, who discovered them
in 1761.

Anglesey (island and county of *Wales, Great Britain*, off north-west
coast)
Not from Angles ey = 'island of the Angles' but from Old Norse onguls
ey = 'island of the strait'. Celtic name was Mon, probably related to Isle
of *Man*.

Angola (Portuguese overseas territory in South-West *Africa*)
From Bantu name Ngola, of unknown meaning but possibly a royal
title.

Anguilla (one of *Leeward Islands, West Indies*)
From Spanish anguila = 'eel'; so named by Columbus in 1493, probably
with reference to its long shape.

Anjou (historic province in west *France*)
From the name of its capital, Angers, in turn from Gaulish tribe Andecavi,
with their own name of Indoeuropean origin = 'water-dwellers'.

Ankara (capital of *Turkey*)
In 7th century BC had Phrygian name Ankire, probably from Indoeuropean ank = 'angled, crooked'. Name is related to English word 'anchor'
and had sense of 'halting place'. Former name of Angora had same origin.

Annapolis (state capital of *Maryland*, USA)
Founded in 1649 as Providence; renamed Annapolis in 1694 after English
princess (later queen) Anne + Greek polis = 'town'.

Antananarivo (former name of *Tananarive, Malagasy Republic*)
Both names are of same origin. Prefix 'an-' indicates location (ie = 'at').

Antarctic (icy landmass and continent surrounding South Pole)
From Greek anti = 'opposite' + *Arctic*.

C

Antibes (port and resort in south *France*, south-west of *Nice*)
Arose in 5th century BC as Greek colony with name of Antipolis = 'opposite the town'; town is on opposite (west) side of bay to *Nice*.

Antigua (one of *Leeward Islands, West Indies*)
Discovered in 1493 by Columbus and named by him after church of Santa Maria la Antigua in *Seville, Spain*. Name of church = 'Saint Mary the Ancient'.

Antilles (alternative name—as Greater and Lesser Antilles—of *West Indies*)
Map of 1424 shows an island in this part of the ocean named Antilias, from Latin ante = 'before, in front of' + illos = 'islands'. After discovery of *America* name spread to all islands lying 'before' the east coast here.

Antioch (city in south *Turkey*)
Founded at end of 4th century BC by Seleucus (general in army of Alexander the Great) who named it after his father Antiochus. Modern (Turkish) name is Antakya.

Antipodes Islands (in *Pacific*, south-east of *New Zealand*)
From Greek antipodes = 'with feet opposite'. Islands are almost exactly on opposite side of world to Greenwich, from where meridian (0°) is measured.

Antwerp (city and port in north *Belgium*)
More likely to be derived from Flemish andwerp = 'dam', than from an der werp = 'by the wharf'. City is on River *Scheldt*.

Aosta (town in north *Italy*, north-west of *Turin*, capital of Valle d'Aosta province)
Founded by Romans in 25 BC and named Augusta Praetoria in honour of Emperor Augustus.

Apennines (mountain chain running down centre of *Italy*)
From Celtic pen = 'peak' (same word as for English Pennines).

Appalachian Mountains (great range of mountains along east coast of North *America*)
Named after Indian tribe of Apalachee or Apalachi, whose territory was here. Name was recorded in 1528 (as Apalachen) as that of Indian province.

Apulia (region in south *Italy*)
From Indoeuropean ap = 'water'; region is low-lying in north and south and borders on *Adriatic*.

Aquitaine (historic province in south-west *France*)
From Latin aqua = 'water'; region is fertile plain bounded on west by Bay of *Biscay* and drained by River *Garonne* and its tributaries.

Arabia (great peninsula in South-West *Asia*)
Probably from Arabic Bilad-al-arab = 'country of plains', or possibly from Arabic arabah = 'desert' (Arabs are desert-dwellers).

Arafura Sea (section of south-west *Pacific*, between *Australia* and *New Guinea*)
Perhaps from native (Galela) halefuru = 'uninhabited region', or from Malay alifura = 'heathens, wild ones', or alfuren = 'forest people'. Name was originally that of island inhabitants here, as well as that of territory where they lived.

Aragon (historic region in north-east *Spain*)
From Celtic or pre-Celtic ar = 'to flow'. Name first applied to River Aragon, tributary of River *Ebro*, then to whole kingdom.

Aral Sea (in republic of *Kazakhstan*, USSR)
From Mongolian aral = 'island', or Kazakh aral = 'bushes', or perhaps Kirghiz aral-dengis = 'island sea'.

Ararat, Mount (in north-east *Turkey*, near frontier with *Armenia*)
Name probably connected with ancient people and country of Urartu (9th–6th centuries BC). Legend links name with story of Armenian king, Ara the Handsome, said to have spurned the love of the Babylonian

princess Shamiram (Semiramida) and suffered defeat from her troops at the foot of this mountain. Turks call it Agri Dag = 'crooked mountain' and Persian name is Kuhi-Nuh = 'Noah's mountain' (according to Bible story, Ark came to rest on mountain).

Archangel (city and seaport on *White Sea*, north-west USSR)
Named after monastery of St Michael the Archangel, founded here in 12th century. City was built in 1584 by order of Ivan IV with original name of Novokholmogory. Name was changed in 1613 to Arkhangelsky and subsequently to present Russian Arkhangelsk.

Arctic (icy landmass and sea surrounding North Pole)
From Greek arktikos = 'northern', in turn from arktos = 'bear' as territory lies under constellation of Great Bear.

Ardennes (forest in south *Belgium*, *Luxembourg* and north-eastern *France*)
From Celtic ard = 'height', + suffix -enna. Latin authors wrote of Arduenna silva.

Argentina (republic in south of South *America*)
In 1526 English explorer Sebastian Cabot, leading Spanish expedition, named the river where he bartered with the Indians for silver Rio de la plata = 'river of silver', not knowing that the silver was not got locally. When country achieved independence in 1826 name became Argentina, from Latin argentina = 'silvery'. (See also *Plate, River*.)

Arizona (state in south USA)
From Indian (Papago) ali = 'little' + shonak = 'spring', ie 'place of the little spring'. Original Spanish name was Arizonac, but 'c' was later dropped to sound more like genuine Spanish name. Original 'little spring' is now south of the border, in *Mexico*.

Arkansas (state in south central USA)
Original name of a river, from Indian Akenzea, of unknown meaning; later became name of whole state. River name was given final 's' to match that of neighbouring state of *Kansas*.

Arles (town in south-west *France*)
From Roman name Arelate, derived from Gaulish ar = 'by' + lait = 'marsh'. Town is situated on low-lying land beside River *Rhône*.

Armenia (republic of USSR south of *Caucasus Mountains*)
Name is ancient, though of uncertain origin. Known as early as 6th century BC. Legend tells of one Armenak, supposed forefather of all Armenians.

Arnhem (city in *Netherlands* on River *Rhine*, south-east of *Utrecht*)
From Roman name Arenacum, in turn from Celtic ar = 'marshland'. (Compare *Arles*.)

Arno, River (river of central *Italy* flowing west through *Florence* and *Pisa* into Ligurian Sea)
From Indoeuropean er = 'to move' or ar = 'to flow'. Sanskrit arna = 'flowing'.

Arras (town in north-east *France*, south-west of *Lille*)
Former capital of Atrebates, whose name derived from root word trebo = 'people'. (See also *Artois*.)

Artois (historic province in north-east *France*)
Roman name was Artesia, from Gaulish tribe of Atrebates, with name = 'people, dwellers' (see *Arras*). (Latin name survives in English 'Artesian well', first adopted here.)

Ascension Island (in South *Atlantic*, midway between *Brazil* and *Angola*)
Discovered by Portuguese in 1501 but then abandoned. Rediscovered by them on Ascension Day, 1508.

Ashkhabad (capital of republic of *Turkmenia*, USSR)
From Turkmenian uskh = 'pleasant' + Iranian abad = 'town'. From 1919 to 1927 was Poltoratsk.

Asia (largest continent in world, east of *Europe*)
From Assyrian asu = 'sunrise, east', in contrast to ereb = 'sunset, west'

(see *Europe*). Originally 'Asu' was only east coast of *Aegean Sea*. Name then spread gradually—in 1st century BC Asia was name of Roman province—to whole continent. (Compare *Levant, Japan*.)

Assam (state in north-east *India*)
In 13th century one of Thai peoples (Ahomi) set up state here called Ahom = 'invincible'. This sounded like 'Assam' to neighbouring tribes and came to denote whole region of valley of River *Brahmaputra*. Not likely to be connected with Sanskrit a-sama = 'incomparable'.

Astrakhan (city and port on delta of River *Volga*, inland from *Caspian Sea*, in south-west USSR)
Of uncertain origin; perhaps from an Iranian language or from Tatar hajji = 'one who has made a pilgrimage to Mecca' + tertkhan = 'high rank awarded by a khan (of the Golden Horde)', giving general sense of 'town belonging to a highly venerated man' (who according to legend was one Asha).

Asturias (historic region in north-west *Spain*)
Named after River Asturia, in turn with name derived from Iberian asta = 'rock' + ura = 'water'.

Asunción (capital of *Paraguay*, South *America*)
Spanish explorers built fort here on 15 August, Feast-day of Assumption, 1536, giving it full name Nuestra Señora de la Asunción = 'Our Lady of the Assumption'. Last word gives present name.

Atacama (desert in South *America*, largely in *Peru* and *Chile*)
From an Indian word = 'desert land'.

Athens (capital of *Greece*)
According to ancient Greeks, city was named after Athene, its patron goddess, but name may be of pre-Greek origin, from language of Pelasgians (who inhabited south part of *Balkan* Peninsula before 3000 BC), with meaning = 'hill, height'.

Athos, Mount (in north-east *Greece*, in *Macedonia*)
Modern Greek name is Hagion Oros = 'holy mountain'. On mountain
is self-governing community of 20 monasteries in which there once lived
nearly 4,000 monks.

Atlanta (state capital of *Georgia*, USA)
Not named directly after *Atlantic Ocean*, but after Western and Atlantic
Railroad, for which town was terminus; name was given in 1845 by rail
engineer J. E. Thomson.

Atlantic Ocean (between *Europe* and *Africa* (west) and *America* (east))
Name given by ancient Greeks after *Atlas Mountains* in north-west
Africa.

Atlas Mountains (North-West *Africa*)
Named by ancient Greeks after legendary giant who stood here bearing
the heavens on his shoulders. Name may possibly have more factual link
with Berber adrar = 'mountain'.

Auckland (city, seaport and former capital of *New Zealand*, on North
Island)
Founded in 1840 and named, even before it was built, after Lord Auckland,
patron of 1st governor Captain William Hobson, who selected city as
capital. Capital transferred to *Wellington* in 1865.

Augsburg (city in south of West *Germany*, north-west of *Munich*)
Founded as Roman fortified town in 12 BC with name Augusta Vindeli-
corum, in honour of Emperor Augustus. (The 2nd word is name of tribe
Vindelicii, possibly meaning 'fortunate ones, fair ones'.) Name was
shortened to 1st element + German suffix burg = 'town'.

Augusta (town and river port in *Georgia*, USA)
Named in honour of Princess Augusta, daughter-in-law of English king
George II (reigned 1727–60).

Austin (state capital of *Texas*, USA)
Named after Stephen F. Austin (1793–1836), Texan coloniser.

Australia (continent and great island between Indian Ocean and *Pacific*)
From Latin australis = 'southern'. Originally Terra Australis Incognita
(= 'unknown southern land') and so marked on Ptolemy's map in 2nd
century AD; then—though still undiscovered—Terra Australis. Northern
coast was sighted by Dutch explorers in 1st half of 17th century and given
name New Holland, but in 1814 English explorer Matthew Flinders proposed return to former name of Terra Australis. Finally, 2nd word, with
ending -ia, became eventual name.

Austria (republic in central *Europe*)
From Latin Marchia austriaca = 'eastern land', the name of one of the
states formed in 9th century after the collapse of Charlemagne's empire.
The 2nd word gives modern name. German name of Österreich has same
basic meaning, from ost = 'east' + Reich = 'kingdom, state'.

Auvergne (historic province in central *France*)
From Roman name Arvernicum, after Gaulish tribe Arverni who inhabited region before Roman conquest of Gaul in 1st century BC. Tribal
name derives from Celtic ar = 'good' + vern = 'warrior'.

Avignon (town in south *France* on River *Rhône*)
Name derives from Roman Avennius, perhaps a personal name, + suffix
(Latin -onem) indicating possession.

Azerbaijan (republic in USSR south-east of *Caucasus Mountains*)
Of uncertain origin. Popular theory is that name means 'land of fire'
(natural combustible gases are found in north, and around them grew
up temples of fire-worshippers).

Azores (islands in North *Atlantic*, west of *Lisbon*, *Portugal*)
From Portuguese Ilhas dos açores = 'islands of hawks'; Portuguese explorers who discovered islands in 1431 noticed a large number of these
birds here. Islands were in fact known earlier to Carthaginians and also
to Arabs and Norsemen, who called them 'Bird Islands'.

Azov, Sea of (arm of *Black Sea*, USSR)
Probably from town of Azov, at mouth of River *Don*. Name of town said

to derive from Polovtsian prince Azum or Azuf, killed when Polovtsy (Turkish nomadic tribe) captured town in 1067.

Baden (region, former state, in south-west of West *Germany*)
As with many German and Swiss towns and spas of similar name, from German bad = 'springs, baths'. (See *Baden-Baden*.) Region forms part of modern 'Land' of *Baden-Württemberg*.

Baden-Baden (famous spa in south-west of West *Germany*, south-west of *Karlsruhe*)
Best-known of the various Badens, so named as it was capital of former state of *Baden*, ie it was the 'Baden' Baden as distinct from any other Baden. Roman name of town was Aquae Aureliae = 'waters of Aurelius', in honour of Emperor Aurelius.

Baden-Württemberg ('Land' in south-west of West *Germany*)
Formed in 1952 from 'Länder' of *Baden*, Württemberg-Baden, and Württemberg-Hohenzollern. (For origin of these see *Baden, Hohenzollern, Württemberg*.)

Badlands (region in South *Dakota*, USA)
Probably translation of French name Terres mauvaises; region is infertile, rocky and desolate.

Baffin Bay (between north-east *Canada* and *Greenland*)
Named in honour of English navigator William Baffin (1584–1622) who discovered bay in 1616 when leading an expedition in search of the North West Passage from the *Atlantic* to the *Pacific*.

Baghdad (capital of *Iraq*)
From Iranian bag = 'God' + dad = 'gift', ie 'God's gift'.

Bahamas (group of islands in *Atlantic*, off south-east *Florida*, USA)
Origin unknown. Bahama was originally the name of a small stream in northern *Cuba*; later the strait between *Cuba* and *Florida* was called the

New Bahama Straits (now the Straits of Florida), and eventually the name of the strait became that of the islands.

Bahia Blanca (city and seaport in *Argentina*, South *America*)
Spanish = 'white bay'. Bay gave name to town.

Bahrain (group of islands in Persian Gulf)
From Arabian bahr = 'sea'. Literally 'two seas', in sense either of a country possessing not one sea but two, or referring to position of islands in between two seas.

Baikal, Lake (in south-east *Siberia*, north of *Mongolia*)
Possibly from a Mongolian word of uncertain meaning, but perhaps from native (Yakut or Buryat) word = 'big'. Chinese name is Pai-hai = 'northern sea'. Early Russian settlers named it Holy Sea.

Baku (capital of republic of *Azerbaijan*, USSR)
Popular theory explains name as deriving from Arabic through Persian with meaning 'windswept' (Persian baadku = 'mountain wind'). Possibly from Iranian abad = 'town' + ku = 'fire' (with reference to practice of fire-worship). True origin still uncertain.

Balaklava (port in south *Crimea*, USSR, on *Black Sea*)
Possibly from Turkish balik = 'fish' + yuva = 'nest'; bay of Balaklava is one of richest fishing areas in *Black Sea*. Or perhaps from former town Palakion, situated here in 2nd–1st centuries BC, named in honour of Palak, son of Scythian king Scilur (although this name was not known before Turks captured town in 1475).

Balaton, Lake (large lake in *Hungary*, south-west of *Budapest*)
Not likely to be derived from Slavonic boltno (Russian boloto) = 'marsh'. Possibly from Illyrian pelso = 'forest'.

Balboa (port at *Pacific* end of *Panama* Canal)
Named after Spanish explorer Vasco Nuñez Balboa (1475–1517) who was 1st European to cross *Panama* isthmus (in 1513) and sight the *Pacific*.

Balearic Islands (off east coast of *Spain*, in *Mediterranean*)
Possibly from Phoenician words = 'islands of the sling' (compare Greek ballein = 'to throw, to sling'), and in fact inhabitants fought for Romans as stone-slingers. But name may be of pre-Phoenician origin.

Balkans (range of mountains in *Bulgaria*)
Name possibly connected with Slavonic balka = 'gorge, ravine', imported by Turkish-speaking Bulgarians from southern *Caucasus*, but borrowed by themselves from Slavs. Or possibly linked with Old Turkish balak = 'high, tall'. Bulgarian name is Stara Planina = 'old mountains'.

Baltic Sea (in northern *Europe*, bounded largely by *Sweden*, *Poland* and north-west USSR)
Of uncertain origin. Roman author Pliny writing in 1st century AD mentions an island called Baltia, from where amber was obtained. Possibly connected with Lithuanian baltas = 'white' or Russian boloto = 'marsh'. Other links could be with Latin balteus, Swedish and Danish balte = 'belt' (in sense of sea 'girding' part of earth).

Baltimore (city and seaport in state of *Maryland*, USA)
Named in honour of English Lord Baltimore, who founded city in 1729 on territory granted to him here by Charles I.

Baluchistan (region of *Pakistan* bounded by *Afghanistan*, Arabian Sea and *Iran*)
From Old Persian = 'land of the tufted-hair folk'.

Bangkok (capital of *Thailand*)
Probably from Bengali bangaung = 'forest village' or perhaps 'olive groves'. Likely to be connected with name of *Bengal*.

Bangladesh (republic between *India* and *Burma*)
From Bengali = 'Bengal nation'. Before 1971 was East *Pakistan*.

Banks Island (most westerly island of North-West Territories, *Canada*, in *Arctic* Ocean)
Discovered in 1819 and named, as are Banks Island, British *Columbia* and

Banks Peninsula, *New Zealand*, in honour of English naturalist Sir Joseph Banks (1743–1820), a member of Cook's 1st expedition.

Barbados (one of *Windward Islands, West Indies*)
Discovered by Spanish explorers, probably in 1518, who named it Los Barbados = 'the bearded', with reference to fig-trees from which hung trails of moss.

Barbary Coast (coast of North *Africa* from *Morocco* to *Libya*)
Named after principal inhabitants, Berbers, whose name has meaning 'man' (ie belonging to one people). Not likely to be connected with English 'barbarian', which derives from Greek barbaros = 'foreign'.

Barcelona (province and its capital in north-east *Spain*)
Said to have been founded by Carthaginian general Hamilcar Barca in 230 BC.

Barents Sea (part of *Arctic* Ocean, bounded by *Norway* and north-west USSR)
Named after Dutch explorer Willem Barents (1550–97) who in 1594 made 1st of 3 attempts to find North-East Passage from *Atlantic* to *Pacific*. He died here, his ship caught in the ice off *Novaya Zemlya*.

Bari (city and seaport on *Adriatic* in province of *Apulia*, south-east *Italy*)
Roman name was Barium, from Latin baris = 'boat, barge' (ie harbour for boats).

Barrow Strait (in north Canada on route from *Baffin Bay* through *Arctic* Ocean to *Beaufort Sea*)
Named in honour of English explorer Sir John Barrow (1764–1843), 1st of the searchers for the North-West Passage. Strait was discovered by Parry in 1819.

Basle (city in north-west *Switzerland*)
Founded in AD 44 as Robur, from Latin roburetum = 'oak grove'. In 374 renamed Basilia, from Greek basileus = 'king': town was fortress for Roman emperor Valentinian I.

Basque Provinces (north-east *Spain*)
Named after Basques, whose own name derives from Basque vasok =
'man' (ie one native to this region and speaking a different language from
surrounding peoples).

Bass Strait (in South *Pacific* between *Australia* and *Tasmania*)
Named in honour of English navigator George Bass who in 1798–9 explored south coast of *Australia* and *Tasmania*.

Basutoland (former name of *Lesotho*)
Named after Basuto or Suto (Sotho) people who are its native inhabitants.
Their name forms main element of *Lesotho*, name of country since 1966.

Bathurst (capital of *Gambia*, West *Africa*)
Named, as are Bathurst, town in *New South Wales*, *Australia*, and Bathurst,
port in north-east *Canada*, after Lord Bathurst, British Colonial Secretary
1812–28. Name changed officially (1973) to Banjul, already in un-
official use amongst natives. Story goes that Portuguese settlers who discovered country in 15th century asked what the place was called, and their
question was misunderstood as 'What are you doing?' Reply was 'Bang-
julo', meaning 'making rope-mats'.

Baton Rouge (state capital of *Louisiana*, USA)
From French bâton rouge = 'red stick'. According to one story, when
French claimed territory here in 17th century they set up a red pole, like
an Indian totem pole, to mark boundary between Indian territory and
their own. Another version says French found pole already existing to
mark boundary between hunting grounds of two Indian tribes. Name
may also perhaps be translation of name of Indian chief.

Bavaria ('Land' in south of West *Germany*)
Named after Germanic tribe Boii, with their own name derived from
Indoeuropean buoi = 'hunting land', who settled here in 6th century AD.

Bayonne (town in south-west *France*, near Bay of *Biscay*)
From Basque baia = 'harbour' + ona = 'good'.

Bayreuth (town in *Bavaria*, West *Germany*, north-east of Nuremberg)
From name of tribe Boii (who gave their name to *Bavaria*) + Old High
German riuti = 'to clear (a wood)', ie 'place cleared by the Boii'.

Beaufort Sea (in *Arctic* Ocean, between north *Alaska* and *Banks Island*)
Named after English admiral Sir Francis Beaufort (1774–1857), hydro-
grapher to Royal Navy (who also gave his name to Beaufort Scale on
which wind speed is measured).

Bechuanaland (former name of *Botswana*)
From name of native inhabitants, Bechuans, with their own name derived
from chuan = 'equal'.

Beira (seaport in *Mozambique*, South-East *Africa*)
Named by Portuguese after Portuguese province of Beira, with meaning
= 'shore'.

Beirut (capital of *Lebanon*)
From Greek berytos = 'wells, springs'.

Belfast (capital of Northern *Ireland*)
From Irish beal feirsde = 'sandy ford'; city is situated at mouth of River
Lagan.

Belfort (town in central eastern *France*, between *Jura* Mountains and
Vosges)
From French bel = 'fine' + fort = 'fortress'. Feature of town is castle on
high rock which was used for defence as recently as 20th century (it
commands route between *Vosges* and *Jura* Mountains).

Belgium (kingdom in north-west *Europe*)
Named after Celtic tribe Belgae, conquered by Caesar in 1st century BC.
They inhabited not only modern Belgium but also *France*. Their name
derives from Celtic belg, bolg = 'brave, warlike'.

Belgrade (capital of *Yugoslavia*)
From Slavonic = 'white city' (probably not literally but symbolically).

Belize (republic in Central *America*, formerly British *Honduras*)
From River Belize, with Indian (Maya) name of uncertain meaning.
Capital from 1970 is *Belmopan*. (Belize was name of capital before this).

Belle Isle (island at east end of strait of same name between *Newfoundland*
and *Labrador*, east *Canada*)
French = 'beautiful island'. Discovered and named by French explorer
Jacques Cartier in 1535, who by sailing through Belle Isle Strait proved
that *Newfoundland* was an island.

Bellingshausen Sea (part of *Pacific* west of *Graham Land*, *Antarctic*)
Named after Russian explorer F. F. Bellingshausen (1778–1852) who led
expedition which discovered sea in 1821.

Belmopan (capital of *Belize*, formerly British *Honduras*)
From name of former capital *Belize*, destroyed by hurricane in 1961,
+ River Mopan, tributary of River Belize, on which it stands. City is
situated 50 miles (80km) inland; founded in 1967, government began
transfer here in 1970.

Belorussia (same as *Byelorussia*)

Benares (city in south-east *Uttar Pradesh*, *India*, on River *Ganges*)
Native name is Varanasi, of which Benares is a corruption. Name derives
from that of River Varana (Barna) and River Asi, which flow into River
Ganges at point where city is situated. Benares is ancient sacred Hindu city,
with flights of steps leading down to river called 'ghats' (see *Ghats*). This
explains false derivation sometimes given—from Sanskrit varanasi =
'town of best water'.

Bengal (historic territory in north-east *India*)
From Hindi Bang-alaya = 'habitation of the Bangs' (who once lived here).

Benghazi (joint capital, with *Tripoli*, of *Libya*, North *Africa*)
Named after Moslem saint Ben-Ghazi (Ben-Rhasi) who is venerated
here and buried near here.

Bergamo (province and city in north *Italy*)
Name is ancient, from Celtic or Ligurian berg = 'mountain'; city is
1,200 feet (365m) above sea level.

Bergen (city and seaport in south-west *Norway*)
From Norwegian Björgvin = 'mountain pasture'.

Bering Sea (part of *Pacific* between *Siberia* and *Alaska*, with Bering
Strait to the north)
Named in memory of Danish navigator Vitus Bering (1680–1741) who
explored territory for Peter the Great of Russia in 1725–8 and who died
on one of the *Komandorskiye Islands* (now named Bering Island). Name
was proposed by G. Foster, member of Cook's expedition, in 1778, but
came into use only in 19th century, before which was known as *Kamchatka* Sea.

Berkeley (city in *California*, USA, near *San Francisco*)
Named in honour of Irish bishop George Berkeley (1685–1753), a pioneer
of American education (Berkeley is a famous university city) and author
of the line 'Westward the course of empire takes its way'. City was
founded in 1865.

Berlin (largest city in *Germany*, politically divided into east and west,
with East Berlin the capital of East *Germany*)
Origin not yet finally established. Many suggestions have been made,
with words from Germanic, Celtic and Slavonic languages proposed with
meanings as varied as 'lake', 'hill', 'dam', 'place of judgement', 'customs
post', 'sandy place', etc, as well as from personal name Berla. First known
as Berlin in 1244.

Bermudas (group of islands in West *Atlantic*, south-east of *New York*,
USA)
Discovered in 1515 by Spanish explorer Juan Bermudez, who named
them 'Islands of devils' (with reference to strong winds). In 1519 renamed
after him in his honour by a Spanish compatriot.

Berne (capital of *Switzerland*)
Origin uncertain; possibly from Indoeuropean ber = 'marshy place'. In attempt to explain name, legend arose of count who, deciding to found the city but not knowing what to call it, met a bear while out hunting and so decided on 'Bear Town' (from German Bär = 'bear').

Berry (historic province in central *France*, south of *Paris*)
From Roman Biturica, after Gaulish tribe Biturigi, with their own name derived from Celtic bith, bed = 'marshland'.

Besançon (city in central east *France* at foot of *Jura* Mountains)
Roman name was Vesontio, from Gaulish beron = 'river'. Besançon was capital of Gaulish tribe Sequani, whose name = 'water-dwellers' (see *Seine*).

Bessarabia (region in USSR with north and south parts in *Ukraine* and main part in *Moldavia*)
Named either after local ruler Bessara or after Wallachian land Basarab, both names deriving from Thracian tribe Bessi who overran it in 7th century.

Bethlehem (1) (town in west *Jordan*, near *Jerusalem*)
From Arabic beit lahm = 'house of bread' (now 'house of meat'), ie situated in fertile plain.

Bethlehem (2) (town in *Pennsylvania*, USA, north-west of *Philadelphia*)
After town in *Jordan*, occurring (in Biblical sense) in a German hymn sung at the founding of the town on 24 December 1741.

Beverly Hills (suburb of west *Los Angeles*, south *California*, USA)
Name suggested from account of 1907 that American president Taft was staying at a place called Beverly Farms. Name was originally Beverly, but from 1911 Beverly Hills. Ultimately derived from English town of Beverley, Yorkshire. American name has assumed connotation of luxury: Beverly Hills is home of film stars.

Bhutan (state in east *Himalayas* bounded by *Tibet, India* and Sikkim)
From Sanskrit Bhyot = 'Tibet' + anta = 'end', ie 'Tibetan frontier'.

Biafra (former independent republic in *Nigeria,* West *Africa*)
State formed in 1967 when East *Nigeria* seceded from *Nigeria,* taking
name from Bight of Biafra, bay between delta of River *Niger* and Cape
Lopez in *Gabon.* Ceased to exist in 1970.

Biarritz (town and resort on Bay of *Biscay,* in south-west *France*)
Name is of Basque origin, perhaps = 'two oaks', or from miarritze =
'cliff'.

Bihar (state in north-east *India*)
From Sanskrit vihara = '(Buddhist) monastery', though not clear whether
territory was named after a town with a famous monastery, or because
it contained many monasteries.

Bilbao (city and seaport in north-west *Spain*)
From Latin bellum vadum = 'good ford'; city is near mouth of River
Nervión.

Birmingham (city in *Alabama,* USA)
Founded in 1871 and named after English city with reference to its iron
and steel industry, for which American town was soon to be noted.

Biscay, Bay of (in North *Atlantic,* off west coast of *France* and north
coast of *Spain*)
From Basque bizkar = 'mountain range', after ancient name Bizkargun
for section of *Pyrenees.* Name originally applied only to south part of
bay.

Bismarck (state capital of North *Dakota,* USA)
Named in 1873 after German chancellor, Otto von Bismarck (1815–
98), as compliment for German financial support for construction of railway here.

Bismarck Archipelago (in South West *Pacific*, east of *New Guinea*)
Discovered by English in 1700 and named New Britain (still the name of the largest island of the group); in 1884 became German protectorate and renamed after Chancellor Otto von Bismarck.

Bizerta (port on *Mediterranean* in *Tunisia*)
City was originally Phoenician outpost Hippo Diarrhytus, in time corrupted to Hippo Zarytus and eventually, under Arab rule, to Bizerta. Roman name was Hippo regius = 'royal fort', after King Hala (Gala) who set up colony here in 1st Punic War (264–41 BC).

Black Forest (mountainous forest in west of West *Germany*)
Translation of German Schwarzwald. 'Black' because mountains are covered with dark-leaved pines. Roman name was Silva Nigra, with same meaning.

Black Sea (between *Europe* and *Asia*, bounded by USSR, *Turkey*, *Bulgaria* and *Romania*)
'Black' not because of colour of water but because stormier than southern seas. Greek name was Pontos Melas, with same meaning, but was also known as Pontos Axinos = 'inhospitable sea, unfriendly sea', 2nd word sounding like ancient Iranian name Ahshaena = 'dark'. From this in turn derived similar-sounding Greek name Pontos Euxinos, but with opposite meaning = 'hospitable sea, friendly sea' (English name was Euxine Sea). Could, however, be 'black' in sense of 'north', as many Asian languages have colour names for different parts of the world (see *Red Sea*).

Blantyre (city in *Malawi*)
Named after birthplace of Scottish explorer Livingstone, Blantyre in Lanarkshire, *Scotland*. City was founded in 1876, 3 years after death of Livingstone while exploring Central *Africa*.

Bloemfontein (capital of *Orange Free State*, South *Africa*)
From Dutch (Boer) = 'flower spring', probably in sense of 'spring among flowers'. Alternative theory, not so likely, is that land belonged to farmer named Jan Bloem.

Blue Mountains (range in south-east *Australia*, in *New South Wales*)
From bluish haze seen on clear days over uplands on which grow dense eucalyptus forests.

Bogotá (capital of *Colombia*, South *America*)
Founded by Spanish explorer Gonzalez de Quesada in 1538 on 6 August, Feast-day of Transfiguration (Spanish Santa Fé, literally = 'holy faith'), with name Santa Fé de Bogotá. Main element of name derives from Indian (Chibcha) chief Bagotta who ruled territory here.

Bohemia (historic kingdom in central *Europe*; province of *Czechoslovakia*)
From Germanic Bai-haimoz = 'land of the Boii' (tribe who settled here, and in *Bavaria*, in 6th century). Their own name derives from Indoeuropean buoi = 'hunters'.

Boise (state capital of *Idaho*, USA)
From French rivière boisée = 'wooded river'; city derives name from that of river on which it stands, also Boise.

Bolivia (republic in central South *America*)
Before 1825, when a Spanish colony, was known as Upper Peru. Liberated from *Spain* in this year by Simon Bolivar (1783–1830) in South American War of Independence, and renamed after him.

Bologna (city and province in central *Italy*)
In 4th century BC known as Bononia, after Boii (see *Bavaria, Bohemia*), with first 'n' later changing to 'l'.

Bombay (largest city in *India*, on west coast)
From name of goddess Mumbadevi, wife of Siva (Shiva), to whom temple was built here. Portuguese explorers of 15th century named city Bombain instead of Mumbain.

Bonn (capital of West *Germany*)
Probably from Celtic bona = 'town', or perhaps with other meaning = 'good'.

Boothia (peninsula in north *Canada*)
Discovered and explored by Sir James Ross in 1829–33, who named it after his Scottish patron Sir Felix Booth. Region was originally called Boothia Felix.

Bordeaux (chief port of south-west *France*)
Latin name was Burdigala, probably from Gaulish tribe Biturigi, though could also be from bordigala, diminutive of bordo (borda) = 'fish-pond'.

Borneo (largest island in *Indonesia*, in Malay Archipelago)
Spanish explorers who discovered it in 1521 named it after *Brunei*, north-west part of island. Indonesians call it Kalimantan, said to mean 'land of mangoes'.

Bornholm (island in *Baltic Sea*, off south-east *Sweden*)
Latin name in 11th century was Hulmo insula, from Danish holm = 'island'. In 13th century was known as Burghaendeholm = 'island of the Burgundii' (a Germanic tribe; for origin of name see *Burgundy*). From 15th century 1st element of name was simplified to Born, which has incidental meaning of 'stream'.

Bosnia (republic in north *Yugoslavia*)
Named after River Bosnia, in turn with name derived from Illyrian bhogi-na = 'flowing'.

Bosporus (strait linking *Black Sea* with Sea of *Marmara*)
From Greek bos poros = 'ox ford' (with which is linked legend of Greek priestess Io, loved by Zeus, who swam across it in the form of a heifer). Name may however be of pre-Greek origin, from Thracian Bos-para, corresponding to Phrygian Bos-poros = 'bright river'.

Boston (state capital of *Massachusetts*, USA)
Founded by English Puritans in 1630 who named it after English town Boston, Lincolnshire, from which many of them had come.

Botany Bay (inlet on coast of *New South Wales*, *Australia*, south of *Sydney*)

Discovered by Cook's expedition in 1770, botanist members of which are said to have found 400 new species of plants here in less than 3 weeks.

Bothnia, Gulf of (in *Baltic Sea*, between *Sweden* and *Finland*)
Named after former region of *Scandinavia* called in what is now *Sweden* Westerbotten = 'west (valley) bottom' and in what is now *Finland* Osterbotten = 'east bottom'. The 2nd element of these two names gave present name of gulf.

Botswana (republic in southern *Africa*)
Named after native inhabitants, Tswana (Chuana), group of Bantu tribes, after whom was also derived name of country before 1966—*Bechuanaland*.

Bougainville (largest of *Solomon Islands*, South West *Pacific*)
Named after French navigator who sighted it in 1768 during his voyage round the world, Louis Antoine Bougainville (1729–1811).

Boulogne (port in north *France*, on English Channel)
Named by Roman emperor Constantine after Italian city Bononia (modern *Bologna*).

Bounty Islands (in South *Pacific*, south-east of South Island, *New Zealand*)
Named after ship *Bounty*, whose captain, British admiral William Bligh, discovered them in 1788.

Bouvet Island (in South *Atlantic*, south-west of *Cape Town*, South *Africa*)
Named after Pierre Bouvet, French naval officer who discovered it in 1739.

Brabant (historic province between *Belgium* and *Netherlands*; modern province in *Belgium*)
From Old High German bracha = 'new land' + bant = 'region'. Name in 751 was Bragobant.

Brahmaputra, River (river in South *Asia*, rising in *China* and flowing through *Pakistan* and *India* into Bay of *Bengal*)
Perhaps from Sanskrit words = 'son of a brahmin', but more likely to be derived from an older, unknown word.

Brandenburg (town in East *Germany*, south-west of *Berlin*)
Originally thought to derive from Slavonic branibor = 'defending forest' (ie dividing Slavonic tribes from Germanic), with German name— = 'burnt town'—as attempt to explain Slavonic name (though could also be vice versa). Most recent theory is that name may derive from Celtic brandobriga = 'peak town', or may possibly be connected with Slavonic root word brenna = 'marshy' + German burg = 'town'. (Yet another— Canadian—theory is that name may be connected with that of Irish missionary Brendan, who converted Slavs to Christianity.)

Brasilia (capital of *Brazil*)
Named after country, Spanish for which is Brasil, + suffix -ia. Before 1960 capital was *Rio de Janeiro*.

Brazil (republic in South *America*)
Named after red dye (in Portuguese braza, from brassa = 'heat, coals') got from brazil-wood. Word itself is probably corruption of some eastern word, as Latin brasilium referred to red dye-wood brought from the East. Brazil was discovered by Portuguese navigator Cabral in 1500.

Brazzaville (capital of *Congo*, Central *Africa*)
Named after Pierre de Brazza (1852–1905), French explorer of Italian extraction who founded it in 1880, + French ville = 'town'.

Bremen (city and port on River *Weser*, north-west of West *Germany*)
From Old High German brem = 'marshy shore'. (Word is related to English 'brim'.)

Brest (city and seaport in west *Brittany*, north-west *France*)
Of uncertain origin. May be connected with later (Breton) name of whole peninsula—Breiz, from Breton bre = 'hill'.

Brindisi (province and port on *Adriatic*, south *Italy*)
Roman name was Brundisium, from Illyrian brentas = 'deer', either because winding coast looked like deer's head with antlers or because deer were once plentiful here (perhaps they had been herded on to one of the headlands).

Brisbane (capital of *Queensland*, *Australia*)
Named in honour of former English governor of *New South Wales*, Sir Thomas Brisbane, who founded it in 1824.

Britain (name used for *Great Britain*)
From Roman name Britannia, from Celtic tribe of Britons who once inhabited south-west *England*. Their own name possibly derives from Celtic brith = 'speckled', from Indoeuropean brit = 'marshy place', or from Phoenician Baratanak = 'land of tin'. (See also *Brittany*.)

Brittany (historic province in north-west *France*)
Name arose in 5th century AD when Britons fled here from *Britain* to escape Germanic invaders (Angles, Saxons and Jutes). Roman name was Britannia minor = 'little Britain', in contrast to Britannia major = 'great Britain'.

Brno (city in *Czechoslovakia*, south-east of *Prague*)
Possibly derives from Roman name Eburodunum, mentioned by Ptolemy writing in 2nd century AD. Other theories: 1. from German Brunnen = 'well, spring'; 2. from Hungarian personal name Burin; 3. from Slavonic brnie = 'mud, clay'.

Broken Hill (town in *New South Wales*, *Australia*)
Great mining town from 1883, when hill on which it stands was first 'broken' to extract rich deposits of silver, lead and zinc.

Brooklyn (borough of *New York* city, USA, on *Long Island*)
Founded by Dutch settlers in 1625 from small town of Breukelen, near *Amsterdam*. Name re-spelt by English who occupied it in 1664.

Brooks Range (mountains in north *Alaska*, USA)
Named after geologist A. H. Brooks, who led survey work here from 1903 to 1924.

Bruges (city in west *Belgium*)
From Dutch brug = 'bridge', possibly in sense of 'town with many bridges', but more likely referring to one bridge by which town arose, as was the case with many towns in Middle Ages.

Brunei (sultanate of north-west *Borneo*, *Malaysia*, and its capital)
From Malay name Berunai with basic meaning = 'plant' (ie mangoes). (See also *Borneo*.)

Brunswick (city in north of West *Germany*, former capital of historic duchy of Brunswick)
From name of Saxon count Bruno + Old High German wik = 'settlement'. German name is Braunschweig, not as close to original name as English.

Brussels (capital of *Belgium*)
From Flemish brock = 'marsh' + sali = 'building', in sense of 'town built on a marsh'; city was originally built on an island in marshes of River Senne, tributary of River *Scheldt*.

Bucharest (capital of *Romania*)
Said to have been founded in 15th century by shepherd named Bucur, but in fact city existed before this. May be connected with Albanian bucur = 'pleasant, beautiful', or with Romanian = 'to rejoice'.

Budapest (capital of *Hungary*)
Name was given to city when two independent towns merged in 1872: Buda, on right bank of River *Danube*, and Pest on left bank. Both names are of Slavonic origin: Buda may = 'building' or 'water'; Pest (Pesht) may = 'cave' or 'hearth'.

Buenos Aires (capital of *Argentina*, South *America*)
Founded by Spanish settlers in 1535 with full name of Ciudad de la Santisima Trinidad y puerto de nuestra señora la virgen Maria de los

buenos aires = 'City of the Most Holy Trinity and port of Our Lady the Virgin Mary of Good Winds'. Name has nothing to do with the climate: 1st half of name was given because city was founded on Trinity Sunday; 2nd half because Virgin Mary was patron saint of sailors (who prayed that she would send favourable winds for their ships). By 19th century only last two words remained as name, and these are today often shortened even further to Baires.

Buffalo (city in *New York* state, USA)
Name given in 1810, either after nearby Buffalo Creek, or after name of Indian chief.

Buganda (region of *Uganda*, East *Africa*)
From name of native inhabitants—Ganda— + prefix bu-. Name of whole country derives from it.

Bulawayo (city in *Rhodesia*, Central *Africa*, south-west of *Salisbury*)
From native Gubulawayo = 'place of killing'; city was founded on site of kraal, burned down in 1893, of Matebele chief Lobenguela.

Bulgaria (republic in south-east *Europe*)
From name of native inhabitants, Bulgars, originally Turkish-speaking tribe in north-west *Caucasus*. Their own name possibly derives from Turkish bul = 'to mix' or Old High German belgh = 'to increase'.

Burgos (province and its capital in north *Spain*)
From Gothic baurgs = 'barricade of wagons, laager'; in 884 a number of settlements united here in their defence against the Arabs.

Burgundy (historic province in east central *France*)
From Germanic tribe Burgundii who settled here in 5th century, with their name derived from Gothic baurg jans = 'dwellers in fortified places'. They had originally settled on *Bornholm*.

Burma (republic in South-east *Asia*)
From Sanskrit mranma, bəma = 'strong ones' (ancient name of native inhabitants). Burmese name for country is Bama.

Burundi (republic in Central *Africa*)
With independence of Ruanda-Urundi in 1962, Burundi (otherwise Urundi) remained a monarchy, while Ruanda (now *Rwanda*) became a republic. Burundi became a republic in 1966, with name derived from majority population, Barundi.

Byelorussia (republic in west USSR)
Otherwise White Russia, from Russian byely = 'white', supposedly because White Russians were originally fair-haired race with light grey eyes who wore white garments. More likely explanation of 'white' is in sense of 'free', with reference to liberation of White Russians from Tatar yoke. Another derivation may be from River Belaya, tributary of River Narev. ('White' has no connection with later Russian meaning of 'counter-revolutionary, anti-Communist'.)

Byrd Land (territory in *Antarctic* between *Bellingshausen Sea* and *Ross Sea*)
Name given in 1929 by American explorer Richard Byrd (1888–1957). Territory was originally named Marie Byrd Land, after explorer's wife.

Cádiz (province and its capital in south *Spain*)
From Phoenician gadir = 'wall', ie city surrounded by walls.

Caen (city in *Normandy*, north *France*)
From Gaulish catu = 'battle' + magos = 'field'.

Cairo (capital of *Egypt*)
English version of last element of Arabic name Misr-al-Kahira = 'Mars the victorious'; city was founded in 969 when *Egypt* was conquered by Arabs, who in 641 had founded El Fustat, now Old Cairo (this name being derived from Byzantine fortress of Fossatum, from Latin fossa = 'moat'). (Planet Mars, god of war, was said to be visible on night city was founded.)

Calabria (region in extreme south of *Italy*)
Possibly from Gaulish root kal = 'white', though not easy to see in what

sense, and perhaps derived from Indoeuropean kal = 'watercourse', as region is mountainous.

Calais (town and seaport in north-east *France* on Straits of Dover)
Named after Belgian/Gaulish tribe Caleti, whose name = 'dwellers by the sea', from Gaulish cul = 'channel'.

Calcutta (2nd largest city in *India* and capital of Western *Bengal*)
Many possible origins: most likely is from Sanskrit Kalikata = 'abode of Kali'—a Hindu goddess, wife of Siva (Shiva).

Calgary (city in south *Alberta, Canada*)
Named in 1876 by Scottish colonel James MacLeod after his native Scottish village of Calgary on Isle of Mull.

California (state in south USA)
True origin uncertain. Said to have been named by Spanish explorer Cortez in 1535, either from Spanish Caliente fornalla (Latin calida fornax) = 'hot furnace', referring to powerful heat of sun, or after legendary isle of Greek mythology ruled by Queen Caliphia. In fact Cortez also named it Santa Cruz = 'holy cross', but this name was already widespread in *America* and did not last.

Calvados (department in north *Normandy*, north *France*)
Named at end of 18th century after ledge of rocks off coast here, in turn from Latin calvus = 'bald' + dossum (French dos) = 'back', referring to reef.

Cambodia (republic in south *Indochina*)
Said to be named after mythical forefather of all Khmers who are its native population—Cambu (which is also name of River *Mekong* in Cambodia). Official name is *Khmer Republic*.

Cameroon (republic in west Central *Africa*)
Named after River Cameroon, in turn with name derived from Portuguese camarões = 'prawns', observed in it by Portuguese sailors who discovered it.

Campania (region in south *Italy*, on *Tyrrhenian Sea*)
From Latin campus = 'field, plain'; region is flat and fertile.

Canada (country occupying almost whole of North *America*, north of USA)
Originally name of one of a number of Indian settlements, then of regions surrounding it, and eventually of whole country. Probably from Indian (Iroquois) kanata = 'cabin, lodge'. Not likely to be from Spanish cañada = 'canyon' or Portuguese = 'path', since neither Spanish nor Portuguese ruled here. During French rule was called New France (French La Nouvelle France).

Canary Isles (in North *Atlantic*, off north-west coast of *Africa*)
Known in ancient times to Phoenician, Greek, Carthaginian and Roman sailors (the latter calling them Insulae Fortunatae = 'fortunate islands'). The 1st 'modern' discovery was by Spanish explorers in 1402 who called them Islas Canarias = 'dog islands', as they had heard of legendary islands in the West said to be populated by men with dogs' heads and, on landing, heard (wild) dogs barking in the woods. Islands in turn have given name to canaries, found as wild birds here.

Canaveral, Cape (former name of Cape *Kennedy*)
From Spanish = 'canebrake' (thicket of reeds), probably referring to cape's appearance as seen from the sea by Spanish sailors in the 16th century. Renamed Cape *Kennedy* in 1963.

Canberra (capital of *Australia*, in *New South Wales*)
Although of recent foundation (1913), origin of name is uncertain. Region where city was founded was named Limestone Plain, but town assumed native name of Canberra. Perhaps derived from aboriginal word = 'meeting-place'.

Cannes (seaport and resort on *Mediterranean* in south *France*)
Probably from Latin canna = 'reed' (French word is plural), or perhaps from pre-Indoeuropean can = 'height'; old town of Cannes is at foot of low hills.

Cantabrian Mountains (north *Spain*)
Named after Cantabri, Iberian tribe defeated in Cantabrian War of 29–19 BC by Augustus.

Canterbury (province on South Island, *New Zealand*)
Named after Canterbury Association, Anglican society (with Archbishop of Canterbury as president) whose members settled here in 1850 with aim of planting colony on similar lines to those of Presbyterian settlement set up two years earlier at *Dunedin*.

Canton (former name of *Kwangchow, China*)
English version is in fact corruption of name of province Kwangtung of which Canton (*Kwangchow*) is the capital.

Cape Province (in south of South *Africa*)
Full name is Cape of Good Hope Province, named (1910) after famous headland here. (Before this was Cape Colony.)

Capetown (capital of South *Africa* and of *Cape Province*)
Founded by Dutch in 1652 with name Kaapstad, of which Capetown is English translation (ie 'Cape of Good Hope Town').

Cape Verde Islands (in *Atlantic* west of *Senegal*, West *Africa*)
Named after Cape Verde (originally Portuguese Cabo Verde = 'green cape') in *Senegal*, to west of which they lie.

Capri (island off coast of *Campania, Italy*, near *Naples*)
Not likely to be derived from Latin capra = 'goat'—this is merely attempt to explain name—but perhaps from Greek kabros = 'boar' (island was former Greek colony), or from Etruscan capra = 'burial ground'.

Carácas (capital of *Venezuela*, South *America*)
Founded by Spanish explorers in 1567 and named after warlike Indian tribe Caracas, with full name of town Sant Jago de Leon de Caracas = 'Saint James of the Lion of the Caracas'.

Cardiff (capital of *Wales, Great Britain*)
From Celtic caer = 'fortress' + personal name Didius (ie 'Didius' castle')
or + Dydd, Welsh name of River Taff on which city stands. (Welsh
name of city is Caerdydd.)

Caribbean Sea (part of *Atlantic* bounded by *West Indies* and coasts of
Central *America, Venezuela* and *Colombia*)
Named after Caribs, Indian tribe with their own name = 'heroes, brave
ones', who inhabited *West Indies* and were encountered by Columbus
when he landed here in 1492. Tribal name is related to English word
'cannibal'.

Carinthia (province in south *Austria*)
Named after Celtic tribe who lived in the *Alps* here BC, with their own
name derived possibly from Illyrian karant = 'rock, cliff', or from Celtic
karantos = 'friendly ones'. German name is Kärnten.

Carolina (two states, North and South, in south-east USA)
French coloniser Jean Ribaut established settlement of Huguenots here
in 1560 and named it in honour of French king Charles IX, with name
La Caroline. With time this name fell out of use, and in 1629 territory
was granted to English coloniser Robert Heath who named it Carolina
after English king Charles I. In 1663 state was re-granted to 9 proprietors
by English king Charles II, for whom name Carolina was just as suitable.
State divided into North and South in 1712, with separate governor for
each.

Caroline Islands (in West *Pacific*, west of *Marshall Islands*)
Spanish explorers who discovered them in 1528 called them Islas de los
Barbados = 'islands of the bearded' (ie Polynesians); in 1542 they became
Islas de los Jardinos = 'islands of the gardens'; finally, in 1686, they re-
ceived their present name, given in honour of Spanish king Charles II.

Carpathian Mountains (in East *Europe*, between *Alps* and *Balkans*)
Name is probably of Thracian/Illyrian origin, either after inhabitants
Carpi or connected with Albanian karpe = 'rock, cliff'.

Carpentaria, Gulf of (in north *Australia*, in *Arafura Sea*)
Named in honour of General Pieter Carpentier, Governor General of
Dutch East Indies, in 1623. Discovered by Tasman in 1606.

Carrara (town in *Tuscany*, north-west *Italy*, near Ligurian Sea)
Probably from Latin quadraria = 'quarry' (town is famous for marble
quarried here), or possibly from pre-Indoeuropean cara = 'rock'.

Carson City (state capital of *Nevada*, USA)
Named in honour of Christopher (Kit) Carson (1809–68), famous fron-
tiersman.

Casablanca, (city and seaport in *Morocco*, North-West *Africa*)
Roman name was Anfa. Portuguese founded Casablanca on site of
Roman city in 1515 with name = 'white house' (Portuguese casa branca).
Present form of name is Spanish casa blanca, with same meaning.

Cascade Range (mountains in north-west USA, parallel to *Pacific*)
Named about 1820 after cascades of River Columbia, which cuts through
it.

Caspian Sea (largest inland sea in world, between south USSR and
Iran)
Named after Caspi, race formerly inhabiting territory south of *Caucasus
Mountains*, with their own name perhaps related to Cushites (ancient
inhabitants of North-East *Africa*) + suffix -pi denoting plural.

Castile (historical province in central and north *Spain*)
From Latin castellum = 'fortress', ie 'land of castles' (built for defence
against Moors).

Catalonia (historical region in north-east *Spain*)
Origin uncertain. Not likely to be derived from Got-Alania, ie from
Goths and Alani.

Catania (province and its capital in east *Sicily*, south *Italy*)
Possibly connected with Phoenician katon = 'small' (ie by comparison

to *Syracuse*), although according to archaeologists original population consisted of Sekeloi (who gave name to *Sicily*), from whose language name is more likely to derive—but with unknown meaning.

Caucasus Mountains (range in south USSR between *Black Sea* and *Caspian Sea*)
Mentioned by Greek classical writers Aeschylus and Herodotus, and explained by Roman author Pliny as deriving from Scythian word = 'snow-white'. Possibly connected with Gothic hauhs = 'height', Avestan kahrkasa and Lithuanian kaukas = 'bump' or, more likely, with Iranian words = 'ice-glittering'.

Cayenne (capital of French *Guiana*, north of South *America*)
French form of *Guiana* (*Guyana*), from Indian word probably = 'respected' (ie 'we who demand respect').

Cayman Islands (north-west of *Jamaica*, *West Indies*)
From caymans (South American kind of alligator) found in *Caribbean* here. Islands are more famous for turtles, and Columbus who discovered them in 1503 named them Islas de las Tortugas = 'islands of turtles'.

Cévennes (mountain range in central south *France*)
From Gaulish cebenna = 'ridge, crest'.

Ceylon (former name of *Sri Lanka*)
Original name was Singhala, from Sinhalese inhabitants, in turn with name derived from Sanskrit sinha = 'lion' (ie in sense of 'brave'). Name changed in 1972 to *Sri Lanka*.

Chad, Lake (bordering on north-east *Nigeria*, Central *Africa*, and state named after it)
Probably from Bornuan word with basic meaning = 'large expanse of water'.

Chamonix (town and resort in *Alps*, east *France*)
From Roman name Campimontium = 'mill field' (from Latin campus =

'field' + molentium = 'mill'). Or possibly from Latin campus munitus = 'fortified field' (because region is naturally protected in valley).

Champagne (historic province in north-east *France*)
From Latin campus = 'field, plain' (French champ). Region is flat, especially in north.

Charleston (1) (city in South *Carolina*, USA)
Named as Charles Town in 1670 in honour of English king Charles II (see *Carolina*); name shortened to Charleston in 1783.

Charleston (2) (state capital of West *Virginia*, USA)
Founded in 1794 as Charlestown, but name soon changed to Charleston; given by founder, George Clendenin, as tribute to his father Charles.

Chartres (city in north *France*, south-west of *Paris*)
Roman name was Autricum, probably from Celtic name of River Autura, but in 4th century was renamed Carnotum, after Carnutes (Gaulish tribe who inhabited this region).

Chatham Islands (in South *Pacific*, south-east of *Wellington, New Zealand*)
Discovered in 1791 by English lieutenant W. R. Broughton, who named them after expedition's ship, the *Chatham*.

Cherbourg (seaport on English Channel, north *France*)
From Roman name Caesaris burgus = 'Caesar's town'.

Chesapeake Bay (large inlet on *Atlantic* coast, USA, off *Maryland* and *Virginia*)
Possibly from Indian (Delaware) k-che-seipogg = 'great salt water', or (Algonquian) che-sipi-oc = 'at big river'; certain element is che = 'big'.

Cheyenne (state capital of *Wyoming*, USA)
From Indian tribal name = 'snakes' (tribe's totemic beast). When *Wyoming* was created as a state in 1868, name was proposed for it but rejected

because of 'unpleasant' meaning. It did become that of state capital, however.

Chicago (2nd largest city in USA, in *Illinois*)
Name found in form Chigagou in French text of 1688; from Indian (Algonquian) word = 'stinking', probably referring either to wild onion growing here, to stench of stagnant water (of marshland round Lake *Michigan*), or to skunk (whose fur is valuable). Origin, as with many Indian words, not certain, but may have been she-kang-ong. Name has never been popular, and when city was founded in 1803 it was named Fort Dearborn, after Henry Dearborn, American Secretary of War. This name was not adopted, however, and from 1830 official name was Chicago.

Chile (republic on west coast of South *America*)
Probably from Indian (Araucanian) chili = 'cold, winter' (not connected with English 'chilly', however). Explanation of name is that Peruvian Incas, who conquered part of country, found climate cool compared to their native equatorial land.

Chimborazo, Mount (inactive volcano in *Andes*, *Ecuador*, South *America*)
Named after River Chimbo + Peruvian rasu = 'snow'; volcano is permanently snow-capped.

China (republic in South-East *Asia*)
Name is of Portuguese origin, introduced from *India* in 16th century, deriving either from Ch'in dynasty of 3rd century BC or from Ji-nan = 'south of the sun'.

Chios (island in *Aegean Sea* belonging to *Greece*, off west coast of *Turkey*)
Turkish name is Sakis-Adasi = 'island of mastic', ie island on which mastic tree grows (whose resin is used for varnish and incense).

Christchurch (city on South Island, *New Zealand*)
Founded in 1851 by John Godley of the Anglican Canterbury Association (see *Canterbury*) and named by him after his college at Oxford, Christ Church.

Christmas Island (in central *Pacific,* just north of equator)
Discovered by Cook on Christmas Day, 1777.

Cincinnati (city in *Ohio,* USA)
Founded in 1788, originally with artificially concocted name Losantiville
(from L for 'Licking' + Latin os = 'mouth' + Greek anti = 'opposite' +
French ville = 'town', ie 'town opposite the mouth of Licking Creek'). In
1790 renamed Cincinnati in honour of General St Clair, President of the
Pennsylvania Society of the Order of Cincinnati, a group of Republican
army officers elected on a system based on that of Roman farmer-general
Lucius Quinctius Cincinnatus.

Ciudad Real (province and its capital in central *Spain*)
Spanish = 'royal city'; founded in mid-13th century by King Alfonso X
of *Castile.*

Clermont-Ferrand (city in central *France,* in *Auvergne*)
In Roman times was Augusta Nemetum, after Emperor Augustus +
name of local Gaulish tribe, with their own name derived from Gaulish
nemeton = 'sanctuary'. In 3rd–4th centuries town was named Arverni,
after Gaulish tribe whose capital it was (see *Auvergne*). Finally, in Middle
Ages, town became Clermont (French clair mont = 'bright mountain'),
a popular French name. This was coupled with Ferrand, name of lord of
nearby castle, in reign of Louis XIII (17th century).

Cleveland (city in *Ohio,* USA)
Founded in 1796 and named after landowner Moses Cleaveland (1754–
1806), who planned it. Name re-spelt without first 'a' from 1832.

Coblenz (city in west of West *Germany,* on River *Rhine*)
From Latin confluentes = 'confluence'; city is situated at point where
River *Moselle* flows into River *Rhine.*

Cochin-China (former French colony of *Indochina*)
From Chinese ko-chin-chin = 'southern China'.

Cocos Islands (in Indian Ocean, north-west of *Perth, Australia*)
Islands are covered with coconut palms. Alternative name for them is *Keeling Islands*.

Cod, Cape (long peninsula in south-east *Massachusetts,* USA)
Discovered in 1602 by English explorer Bartholomew Gosnold, who recorded 'near this cape . . . we took great store of codfish'.

Cologne (3rd largest city in West *Germany,* on River *Rhine*)
From Latin Colonia Claudia Agrippina = 'colony of Claudia Agrippina' (wife—and murderess—of Roman emperor Claudius, and mother of Nero), who ordered a fort to be built here in AD 50. City was founded in 38 BC by Roman general Agrippa.

Colombia (republic in north-west of South *America*)
Coast here said to have been visited by Columbus in 1502, after whom country was named in 1863. Spanish settlers of 16th century had called it New Granada.

Colombo (capital of *Sri Lanka*)
Probably from Sinhalese korumbu = 'harbour', though possibly from Kalantotta = 'ford over the (River) Kalan'. City is just south of mouth of River Kelani.

Colón (2nd largest city in *Panama,* Central *America*)
Name in Spanish = 'Columbus' (in sense of 'Columbus's town'). Founded in 1850 with name Aspinwall, after one of railway builders. Renamed Colón in 1890.

Colorado (state in west USA)
State named after River Colorado, in turn from Spanish Rio Colorado = 'red river' (waters are reddish with clay washed down from canyons).

Columbia, District of (in east USA, with capital *Washington*)
Named in 1791 in honour of Columbus. Also named after him are Columbia, capital of South *Carolina* (1786), River Columbia in north-

69

west USA (1792) and British Columbia (1858). (See also *Columbia, Colón, Columbus.*)

Columbus (state capital of *Ohio*, USA)
Named in honour of Columbus in 1812. City of same name in *Georgia* was named in 1828.

Como (lake and city in north *Italy*)
From Celtic camb, comb = 'valley' (compare English 'coomb', Welsh 'cwm').

Comoro Islands (in Indian Ocean, between north *Mozambique* and north *Madagascar*)
Original Greek name, mentioned by Ptolemy in 2nd century AD was Ore Seleniae = 'moon mountains' (Latin montes Lunae). Arabic translation of this is Jebel-el-Komr (Arabic komr = 'moon'), from last element of which comes present name. Islands are associated with moon worship.

Concepción (city in south *Chile*; city in *Paraguay*, South *America*)
Spanish = 'Conception': both cities were founded on 8 December, Feast of Immaculate Conception (1st city in 1550 by Pedro de Valvivia on a site 7 miles (11km) north-east of present city).

Concord (state capital of *New Hampshire*, USA)
Founded in 1725 as Pennycook, from Indian (Algonquian) word probably = 'descent'. In 1763 renamed Concord after city of same name in *Massachusetts*, whose immigrants settled it. Name may have been given to mark peaceful agreement drawn up between two factions.

Coney Island (resort in south-west of *Long Island*, *New York* City, USA)
From English version of Dutch konijn = 'rabbit'; animals once bred and lived here in natural state.

Congo, River (great river in Central *Africa* and republic there)
Republic named after river, in turn named probably from Bantu kong = 'mountains' (through which it flows).

Connecticut (state in *New England*, north-east USA)
From Indian (Algonquian) kuenihtekot = 'long river'. River gave name
to state. The 2nd 'c', which is silent, was probably inserted by an English
scribe thinking of word 'connect'.

Constance, Lake (bordering on *Austria*, West *Germany* and *Switzerland*)
Named after town of Constance, in turn with name derived from Roman
Constantia, after Emperor Constantine I. German name of lake is Boden-
see, from German Boden = 'bottom' (in sense of 'low-lying valley') +
See = 'lake'.

Constantinople (former name of *Istanbul*)
Founded, as New Rome, by Constantine the Great in AD 330 as capital
of Roman empire on site of ancient Byzantium. Name therefore derives
from Constantine + Greek polis = 'town'. Renamed *Istanbul* in 1930.

Cook Islands (in South *Pacific*, east of *Tonga*)
Named in honour of Cook, who discovered some of them in 1773.

Copenhagen (capital of *Denmark*)
From Danish kiopman = 'merchant' + havn = 'harbour', ie 'merchants'
harbour'.

Cordova (province and its capital in *Andalusia*, south *Spain*)
Possibly from Arabic karta-tuba = 'big town'.

Corfu (island and town on it in *Ionian Sea*, off west coast of *Greece*)
Probably from Greek name Kerkyra = 'winding' (referring to its coast),
or possibly from *Cyprus*, from Greek kerkuros = 'boat' (originally name
of bay on east Corfu).

Corinth (town and port on Gulf of Corinth, west of *Athens*, south
Greece)
Has been explained as deriving from Greek korone = 'crown' (ie mountain peak), but name is of pre-Greek origin. Modern Corinth was founded
in 1858 on site of ancient Corinth, which was founded about 1350 BC.

Cork (county and its capital in *Ireland*, on south coast)
From Irish corcaigh = 'marsh', on edge of which town was founded in
7th century.

Corsica (island in *Mediterranean*, north of *Sardinia*)
True origin uncertain: possibly from Phoenician horsi = 'wooded'
(Phoenicians built their ships from wood out of Corsican pine forests),
or perhaps from Greek name Kyrnos, from Phoenician keren = 'horn,
cape, rock', or again perhaps from tribe of Corsi who lived here.

Cortina d'Ampezzo (resort on slopes of *Alps*, north *Italy*)
From Italian cortina = 'yard, smallholding' + dialect word ampezzo,
from Italian in pezzo = 'in the field', ie 'smallholding in the field'.

Corunna (province and its capital in *Galicia*, north-west *Spain*)
Not likely to be from Latin columna = 'column', referring to Roman
Tower of Hercules off Cape Corunna, a famous lighthouse. Probably
from medieval name Coronium, although Roman name was Brigantium.

Costa Blanca (coast of east *Spain* between *Alicante* and *Valencia*)
Spanish = 'white coast' (referring to light-coloured sand).

Costa Brava (coast of east *Spain* from French frontier to *Barcelona*)
Spanish = 'wild coast' (referring to rugged coastline).

Costa del Sol (coast of south *Spain* with *Málaga* as its central resort)
Spanish = 'sunny coast' (ie the Spanish Riviera).

Costa Dorada (coast of west *Spain* from *Barcelona* to *Valencia*)
Spanish = 'golden coast' (with abundance of sun and sand).

Costa Rica (republic in Central *America*)
Spanish = 'rich coast'. When Columbus landed here in 1502 he named
the region Costa del Oro = 'coast of gold' because of gold ornaments
worn by natives and offered to him as gifts.

Costa Smeralda (coast of north-east *Sardinia*)
Italian = 'emerald coast' (from bright green vegetation).

Costa Verde (coast of north *Spain*, extending west from French frontier
to *Corunna*)
Spanish = 'green coast'; region is green and fertile.

Côte d'Argent (coast of south-west *France*, on Bay of *Biscay*, between
Biarritz and mouth of River Adour)
French = 'silver coast' (from brightness of sand, sun and sea).

Côte d'Azur (south coast of *France*, on *Mediterranean*, from Italian frontier westwards to *Marseilles*)
French = 'azure coast' (from deep blue colour of sea and sky); otherwise
the (French) *Riviera*.

Côte d'Émeraude (coast of north *Brittany*, *France*, centring on *Dinard*
and *St Malo*)
French = 'emerald coast' (from colour of sea here).

Côte de Nuits (north region of *Côte d'Or*, *France*)
From French côte = 'hill, slope' + name of town Nuits-St Georges, first
element of which is of uncertain origin: not French = 'nights' but perhaps from Latin nauda = 'marshy place'.

Côte d'Or (plateau in *Burgundy*, central *France*)
French = 'golden slope' (region is famous for vineyards).

Côte Vermeille (section of coast of south *France* adjoining Spanish
frontier)
French = 'vermilion coast' (from bright red colour of rocks and earth).

Cotopaxi, Mount (highest active volcano in world, in *Andes*, *Ecuador*,
South *America*)
From Indian (Quecha) cotto = 'mass, mountain' + pacsi = 'shine, bril-
liance', ie 'shining mountain' (though this may be attempt to explain
older name of unknown meaning).

Cremona (town in *Lombardy*, north *Italy*, south-east of *Milan* on River *Po*)
From Celtic tribe Cenomani, whose own name derives from Celtic cen = 'ridge, crest'.

Crete (island in *Mediterranean*, to south of *Aegean Sea*)
Name is very old, from tribe that once inhabited island. May be connected with Candia, former capital (present Heraklion, Iraklion), and originally name of canal dug in AD 820. Name spread to town and then perhaps by Venetians to whole island.

Crimea (peninsula on north side of *Black Sea*, USSR)
Many possible explanations: most likely is from Stary Krym or Solkhat, former capital of khanate here (though name of town is of unknown origin), or possibly from Turkish kurum = 'ditch, moat' (narrow isthmus at head of peninsula had channel dug across it). Other less likely derivations are: 1. from Turkish kerman = 'fortress'; 2. from Mongolian herem = 'rampart'; 3. from some Russian word such as kroma = 'boundary' or kremen = 'flint'.

Croatia (republic in north-west *Yugoslavia*)
From Croats, who settled here in 7th century AD, with their own name of uncertain origin; perhaps derived from sharvatas = 'armed' or Slavonic gor = 'mountain', or connected with the name of *Carpathians*.

Crozet Islands (in south-west Indian Ocean, south of *Madagascar*)
Discovered in 1772 by French captain Crozet.

Cuba (island republic in *West Indies*, Central *America*)
Was originally name of settlement on island, noted by Columbus in 1492. Name is from (extinct) Indian language of unknown meaning (though 'district' has been suggested).

Curaçao (island in *West Indies*, off north coast of *Venezuela*)
Discovered by Spanish explorer Hojeda in 1449 who called it Isla de los Gigantes = 'island of giants'. Later, in 1499, Spanish colonisers abandoned here several sailors suffering from malaria; some years later another

Spanish expedition was surprised to find them recovered and living among native Indian inhabitants. Island therefore has name derived from Spanish curacion = 'cure'.

Cyprus (island republic in *Mediterranean*, south of *Turkey*)
Possibly from groves of cypress trees, imported here from *Lebanon*. Famous in ancient times for its copper mines; Greek name for island, Kypros, is related to English 'copper'.

Czechoslovakia (republic in central *Europe*)
Name of country formed in 1918 from two main groups of inhabitants, Czechs and Slovaks. Czechs derive their name from Czech četa = 'body of men, army'. (For Slovaks see *Yugoslavia*.)

Dacca (capital of *Bangladesh*)
Named after Durga, wife of Siva (Shiva) and goddess of fertility.

Dahomey (republic in Central West *Africa*, on Gulf of *Guinea*)
Probably from personal name Dag + west Sudanese word = 'inside, intestines'. Negro prince Dag had his belly ripped open by member of his retinue in 17th century and capital was named 'Dag's belly', possibly with metaphorical sense of 'inside Dag' (ie 'in possession of Dag').

Dairen (former name of *Talien*)
Japanese variant of *Talien* (former Russian name being *Dalny*); now, with *Lushun*, forms great port of *Lü-ta, China*.

Dakar (capital of *Senegal*, Central West *Africa*)
Probably from African (Wolof) word = 'waterless'. City was built on volcanic rocks in 1857.

Dakota (two states, North and South, in north USA)
From name of Indian (Sioux) tribe who once inhabited region here. Indian (Omaha) dakota = 'allies', ie members of tribal union. State divided into North and South in 1889.

Dallas (city in north *Texas*, USA)
Named in 1845 after George M. Dallas, Vice-President of USA 1845-9.

Dalmatia (strip of *Adriatic* coast in *Croatia, Yugoslavia*)
Formerly (BC) Illyria. Then named Dalmatia after town Dalmion, with name perhaps connected with Albanian dalmium = 'sheep pasture'. As Roman province, under Augustus, was officially Illyricum, but Dalmatia was name that prevailed.

Dalny (former name of *Talien*)
From Russian = 'far, distant'; port was founded in 1860 in extreme east of Russian empire.

Damascus (capital of *Syria*)
Name is very old and has been known at least 3,000 years, but meaning is uncertain. Perhaps = 'industrious'.

Dampier Archipelago (off north-west coast of Western *Australia*)
Named in 1803 after English explorer William Dampier (1652-1715) who discovered them in 1699. Mountains in South Island, *New Zealand*, are also named after him.

Danube, River (2nd longest river in *Europe*, flowing generally south-east through 8 countries, into *Black Sea*)
Possibly from Sanskrit danus = 'damp', or from Avestan danu = 'current'. From same root as River *Don*.

Dardanelles (strait connecting *Aegean Sea* with Sea of *Marmara, Turkey*)
Formerly Hellespont (Greek = 'Hella's bridge'). From Greek town of Dardanus, in turn named after its inhabitants, with name perhaps connected with Albanian dardhe = 'pear' (though this may be a mere coincidence and connection is hard to see).

Dar-es-Salaam (capital of *Tanzania*, Central *Africa*)
From Arabic = 'house of peace', ie place where merchants could trade freely.

Darjeeling (town in West *Bengal*, north *India*, north of *Calcutta*)
Many unlikely explanations of meaning, as 'far island of meditation',
'land of the lama's sceptre', 'place of thunder' and 'region of precious
stones'. Most likely derivation is from Tibetan dar = 'spread' + gjas =
'broad' + ling = 'island, land', ie 'far spreading land'.

Darling, River (longest tributary of *Murray* River, *Australia*)
Named in 1828 by Captain C. Stewart, first European to sight it, after
Sir Ralph Darling, Governor of *New South Wales*, 1825–31.

Darmstadt (city in central West *Germany*, south of *Frankfurt*)
In 8th century was Darmundestadt = 'town of Darmund' (personal name
in itself shortened from Darmundolf). Then, through similarity of 2nd
element of name with German Munde = 'mouth', came to mean 'town
at the mouth of the Darm', but River Darm was first recorded only in
1759.

Darwin (capital of Northern Territory, *Australia*)
Founded in 1869; at first named Palmerston, after English prime minister
(1784–1865), but in 1911 renamed in honour of Charles Darwin, who had
visited coast here in 1836 on his voyage to *New South Wales*.

Dauphiné (historic province in south-east *France*)
Ceded to French king Philip VI in 1349 when it became official property
(appanage) of king's eldest son, Charles of Valois (future king Charles V),
heir to the throne, who had title of 'dauphin' (from family name, Del-
phinus, of lords of Valois, whose crest had dolphins).

Davis Strait (in North *Atlantic*, between *Baffin Island*, *Canada*, and *Greenland*)
Named after English explorer John Davis (1550–1605) who discovered it
in 1587 when in search of the North West Passage from the *Atlantic* to the
Pacific.

Davos (resort in east *Switzerland*)
From Romansch davo = 'behind'; valley in which town lies turns and

goes back to north, thus sheltering it from wind. So named in 13th century by huntsmen of Baron von Vatz, who discovered it.

Dawson (former capital of *Yukon* territory, north-west *Canada*)
Founded in 1896 in *Klondike* gold rush; named after Canadian explorer and geologist George M. Dawson. Now a 'ghost' town; population at height of gold rush was 25,000—in 1966 only 881.

Dayton (city in state of *Ohio*, USA)
Named after one of founders, Jonathan Dayton (1760–1824). Town first settled in 1796.

Dead Sea (between *Israel* and *Jordan*)
Contains no organic life because of high salt content.

Death Valley (in east *California* and south *Nevada*, USA)
Named in 1849 by party of gold-seeking 'forty-niners', some of whom died of thirst and exposure when trying to cross it.

Deauville (resort in *Calvados* department, north *France*)
Probably from Latin de = 'belonging to' + Germanic auwa = 'damp plain' + Latin villa = 'village'.

Deccan (plateau of south peninsula of *India* between Eastern and Western *Ghats*)
From Sanskrit dakshina-patkha = 'southern country', original meaning being 'right road'. (Compare similar change of meaning in *Yemen*, where 'right' = 'southern' and *Norway*, where 'way' ('road') = 'country'.

Delaware (state on east coast of USA)
Named after Delaware River and Bay, in turn named in honour of Thomas West, Lord de la Warr (1577–1618), appointed Governor of *Virginia* in 1609. (Bay was named by Sir Robert Carr in 1644.)

Delft (town in south *Netherlands*, south-east of *The Hague*)
From Old Dutch delf = 'canal' (word is related to English 'delve'): town is on Schie canal.

Delhi (capital of *India*, and union territory in north *India*)
Founded in 10th century on site of ancient city of Indraprastha. Name is
of uncertain origin, although Hindi dilli = 'threshold' (perhaps with
reference to Hindustan). Old Delhi is also called Shahjahanabad, after
Mogul emperor Shah Jahan who rebuilt it in 17th century. New Delhi,
just south of Old Delhi, was chosen as capital in 1912 and became capital
in 1947.

Denmark (kingdom in north *Europe*)
Named after Germanic tribe, Danes + mark = 'territory'. Danes derive
their name from Old High German tenar (Sanskrit dhann) = 'sandbank'.

Denver (state capital of *Colorado*, USA)
Founded as gold-mining centre in 1858 with Latin name Auraria =
'golden'. Following year renamed Denver in honour of General James W.
Denver, governor of the territory.

Des Moines (state capital of *Iowa*, USA)
City named after river, in turn from French Rivière des moines = 'river
of the monks', perhaps with reference to Trappist monks who had
settled here or, more likely, from name of Indian tribe, recorded in
French text of 1673 as Moingouena, shortened to (plural) Moings.

Detroit (city in *Michigan*, USA)
From French détroit = 'strait', referring to narrow sound between Lake
St Clair and Lake *Erie*. City was founded by French settlers in 1701,
with name probably translated from Indian.

Dieppe (port and resort on English Channel, north-east *France*)
Name related to Flemish dieb = 'deep', referring to mouth of River
Arques on which town is situated.

Dijon (city in central east *France*)
From Roman name Diviodunum = 'hill of Divio'; 2nd element of
name is Celtic.

Dinard (resort on English Channel in north *Brittany, France*)
From Celtic din = 'hill' + (perhaps) Breton arzh = 'bear'.

Dnieper, River (river in USSR flowing south and west through *Ukraine* into *Black Sea*)
Latin name was Danapris, from Sarmatic don = 'river' + ipr (probably also) = 'river'.

Dniester, River (river in USSR rising in *Carpathians* and flowing south-east through *Ukraine* into *Black Sea*)
Latin name was Danaster, from Sarmatic don, dan = 'river' + (probably) Indoeuropean is-ro = 'to flow'.

Dodecanese (group of islands in south-east *Aegean Sea*)
From Greek = 'twelve islands' (dodeka = 'twelve', nesos = 'island'). Largest island in group is *Rhodes*.

Dogger Bank (sandbank in *North Sea*, east of north *England*)
Named after 'doggers'—two-masted Dutch fishing vessels which formerly used region as one of their chief fishing grounds.

Dolomites (region of *Alps* in south-east *Tyrol*, north *Italy*)
Named after French mineralogist Dieudonné de Dolomieu (1750–1801) who carried out extensive work here.

Dominica (one of *Windward Islands, West Indies*)
So named by Columbus, who discovered it on Sunday (Latin (dies) dominica) 3 November 1493.

Dominican Republic (east part of island of *Hispaniola, West Indies*)
In 1697 named Santo Domingo (Spanish = 'holy Sunday'), its capital from 1844, but originally settled by Spanish explorers on a Sunday (see *Dominica*) in 1496.

Don, River (river in USSR flowing into Sea of *Azov*, north of *Black Sea*)
From Sarmatic dan, don = 'river'. Word appears as chief element in

name of a number of rivers, eg *Danube, Dnieper, Dniester* (and English River Don).

Dordogne (department and river in central south *France*)
Probably from Celtic dour = 'river'.

Dortmund (city and port in West *Germany*, north-east of *Essen*)
In 890 was known as Throtmenni, from name of channel, in turn derived from Old High German word = 'throat'. Not likely to be connected with Old High German tros = 'heath', and certainly not = 'mouth of the Dort' as no such river exists.

Douai (town in north-east *France*, south of *Lille*)
Of uncertain origin. Perhaps from Gaulish personal name Dous.

Drakensberg (chief mountain range of South *Africa*)
From Dutch drake = 'dragon' (from wild and dangerous nature of mountains) + berg = 'mountain'. Native name is Quathlamba = 'piled-up rocks'.

Dresden (city in south of East *Germany*)
Named after Slavonic tribe, Drezhdane, with their own name from Slavonic drezga = 'forest' + ending -ane = 'dwellers'.

Dublin (capital of *Ireland*)
From Irish dubh = 'black' + lind = 'lake' (equivalent to English Blackpool). Irish name is Baile Átha Cliath = 'place of the hurdle ford'.

Dubrovnik (resort and seaport in *Dalmatia*, west *Yugoslavia*)
From Slavonic dubrova = 'oak wood'. Older name Ragusa does not derive from Slavonic rogoza = 'reed-mace' (kind of tall grass) but from earlier form Rausim, of unknown origin.

Dunedin (city and seaport on south-east coast of South Island, *New Zealand*)
Founded in 1848 by Scottish Presbyterian settlers, who first wished to call town New Edinburgh. Provost of *Edinburgh*, publisher Sir William

Chambers, then suggested name Dunedin, old Celtic name of *Edinburgh*, with original meaning of 'Edin's fort'.

Dunkirk (port in north-east *France*, on *North Sea*)
From Flemish duine = 'dune' + kerk = 'church', ie 'church on the dunes'. Town grew up round church of St Éloi, built here in 7th century.

Durban (city and seaport in *Natal*, South *Africa*)
Founded in 1824 as Port Natal, after former name of Durban Bay, originally sighted by Portuguese explorer Vasco da Gama on Christmas Day (Portuguese Natale) 1497. In 1835 renamed Port D'Urban, later simplified to Durban, after Sir Benjamin D'Urban, Governor of Cape Colony (1777–1849).

Dushanbe (capital of republic of *Tadzhikistan*, USSR)
Probably named after village on this site in 7th century with same name—Tadzhik = 'Monday' (ie market day). From 1929 to 1961 was Stalinabad (= 'Stalin town').

Düsseldorf (city in west of West *Germany*, on River *Rhine*)
City is situated at point where small River Düssel (with name perhaps from Celtic dur = 'river') flows into River *Rhine*, + German Dorf = 'village'.

E **Easter Island** (in South *Pacific*, west of *Chile*)
Discovered by Dutch navigator Roggeween on Easter Sunday (or possibly Monday) 1722 (although English pirate Edward Davis claimed to have landed here in 1695).

East London (seaport in *Cape Province*, South *Africa*)
Town lies on east coast and is named after British capital *London*. Earlier name was Port Rex, after George Rex, said to be illegitimate son of English king George III. Name changed to East London in 1847.

Ebro, River (river in north *Spain* flowing south-east into *Mediterranean*)
From Roman name Iberus, in turn from Basque ebr, Celtic iber = 'river'. (See also *Iberia*.)

Ecuador (republic on north-west coast of South *America*)
Before 1830 name was *Quito*, that of present capital. Since then called
Ecuador—Spanish = 'equator' (which crosses it).

Edam (town in north *Netherlands*, north-east of *Amsterdam*)
From Dutch = 'dam on the (River) Ee'. (Compare *Amsterdam, Rotterdam*).

Edinburgh (capital of *Scotland, Great Britain*)
Popular explanation is that city was founded in 617 as fortress for Edwin,
King of Northumbria, with name = 'Edwin's (Edin's) castle'. (Compare
Dunedin.) More recent theory says name derives from Eidyn = 'steep
slope', on which was situated din (= 'fortress') of ancient kingdom of
Manau Gododdin in 6th century.

Edmonton (capital of province of *Alberta, Canada*)
Named in 1877 after Fort Edmonton, built in 1795 about 18 miles (30km)
further down River *Saskatchewan*. Fort, which was destroyed by Indians
in 1807 and rebuilt following year where Edmonton now is, was in
turn named by George Sutherland of Hudson Bay Company after Edmonton near *London, England*, probably as compliment to his clerk, Prudens,
who was born there.

Edward, Lake (between *Zaire* and *Uganda, Africa*)
Discovered by English explorer H. M. Stanley in 1888 and named after
Prince of Wales, later King Edward VII. Now Lake Idi Amin Dada.

Egmont, Mount (extinct volcano in west of North Island, *New Zealand*)
Named by Cook in 1770 in honour of English Earl of Egmont, First
Lord of Admiralty. Native name, Taranaki, is used for surrounding
province.

Egypt (republic in North-East *Africa*)
Possibly from Ga-Ka-Pta = 'house of the god Pta' (patron god of ancient
capital Memphis), or from Phoenician kapthor = 'island' (ie surrounded
by waters of River *Nile*), or from Greek aia koptos = 'land of the Copts'.

More likely derivation is from Arabic kemi = 'black land' (with 'black' referring either to colour of inhabitants' skin, waters of *Nile*, or earth). In 1958 official name became United Arab Republic, and from 1972 Arab Republic of *Egypt*.

Eire (alternative name for *Ireland*)

Elba (island off west coast of *Italy*, east of north *Corsica*)
Greek name was Athalia = 'sparkling', then Latin Ilva from which modern form of name, Elba.

Elbe, River (river in Central *Europe* flowing through *Germany* into *North Sea*)
From Indoeuropean alb = 'to go, to flow', from which Scandinavian elv = 'river'. Or possibly from Indoeuropean alb = 'white'.

Elbruz (extinct volcano, highest mountain in *Caucasus*, USSR)
Perhaps from Iranian aitibares = 'high mountain', but more likely from Iranian = 'sparkling' (referring to snows in the sun). Armenian name is Alberis, which may be connected with name of *Alps*.

Élisabethville (former name of Lubumbashi, *Zaire*)
Founded in 1910 and named after Belgian queen Élisabeth, wife of King Albert I, + French ville = 'town'. Renamed Lubumbashi in 1966.

Elizabeth (city in state of *New Jersey*, USA)
Called Elizabethtown until 1740. Named after wife of Sir George Carteret, who founded it in 1664 (also perhaps with reference to Castle Elizabeth, *Jersey*, from which island Carteret had come).

Ellesmere Isle (in *Arctic*, north *Canada*)
Named after Earl of Ellesmere by Sir E. A. Inglefield, who first explored it in 1852.

Ellice Islands (in South *Pacific*, between *Fiji* and *Gilbert Islands*)
Named after head of Canadian shipping firm, Alexander Ellice, who

owned ship *Rebecca* on board which Captain de Peyster discovered them in 1819.

Ellis (small island in *New York* Bay, USA)
Named after Samuel Ellis, *Manhattan* merchant who bought it in 18th century.

El Salvador (alternative name for *Salvador*)
Spanish = 'the Saviour'.

Endeavour Strait (south part of *Torres Strait* between Cape *York*, *Queensland*, *Australia*, and *Prince of Wales Island*)
Named after Cook's ship *Endeavour* which passed through strait on his return voyage in 1770.

Enderby Land (most westerly part of Australian Dependency, *Antarctic*)
Discovered in 1831 by John Biscoe, who named it after English whaling firm of Samuel Enderby & Sons who had financed his expedition.

England (south and chief part of *Great Britain*)
Named after Germanic tribe of Angles who invaded country and settled here in 5th–6th centuries AD. Angles derive their name from Old High German angul = 'angle, corner': they came from 'corner' of what is now extreme north *Germany*, between Flensburg Fjord and River Schlei.

Erebus, Mount (active volcano on Ross Island in Ross Sea, *Ross Dependency*, *Antarctic*)
Discovered by Sir James Ross in 1841 and named after one of expedition's two ships, the *Erebus* (name of legendary Greek god, personification of darkness). Other ship, the *Terror*, gave her name to another volcano here.

Erevan (alternative spelling of *Yerevan*)

Erie, Lake (one of Great Lakes between USA and *Canada*)
Named after Indian (Iroquois) tribe who once inhabited territory round lake. Their name = 'cat', tribe's totemic animal.

Eritrea (territory in *Ethiopia* bordering on *Red Sea*)
From Greek eritros = 'red', referring either to *Red Sea* or to colour of soil.

Esbjerg (port on *North Sea* in south-west *Denmark*)
Possibly from Danish = 'fish bait' or 'mountain range', but more likely corruption of Eskebjerg = 'ash-tree hill'.

Escorial (small town north-west of *Madrid, Spain*)
From Spanish escoria = 'slag, clinker', ie piles of slag left from old mine-workings. Town is famous for fine buildings and art treasures.

Essen (city in north-west of West *Germany*)
In 897 was known as Astnida = 'hills, smelting furnace', from Indo-european as = 'to dry, to burn', with name changing gradually from this to present form. Explanation of meaning is difficult: perhaps in sense of 'woodland cleared by burning'.

Estonia (republic in north-west USSR, on Gulf of *Finland*)
From Esthes, ancestors of modern Estonians. They were a Finno-Ugrian people with name probably derived from Baltic word aueist = 'dwellers by the water'.

Estremadura (historic region in west *Spain*; province in west *Portugal*)
From name of Roman province Extrema Durii, from Latin extremum ab Duera = 'land' farthest from the (River) Duero'. Roman territory on Spanish Peninsula extended from *Mediterranean*, so Estremadura was at its western extremity.

Ethiopia (independent empire in North-East *Africa*)
From Greek aithos = 'burnt' + ops = 'face', ie 'people with sunburnt faces'.

Etna, Mount (highest volcano in *Europe*, in east *Sicily*, south *Italy*)
From Greek aitho = 'to burn'. Sicilian name is Mongibello, probably related to Italian monte bello = 'beautiful mountain' and to Arabic jebel = 'mountain'.

Euphrates, River (river in South-west *Asia*, joining River *Tigris* in *Iraq* to flow into Persian Gulf)
Assyrian name was Purattu, possibly from bur = 'vessel' or, more likely, from ur = 'river', + at = 'father, powerful', ie in sense of 'father of rivers' or 'mighty river'. Or perhaps from cuneiform U-fratus = 'very broad'.

Eurasia (*Europe* and *Asia* regarded as one continent)
From Eur(ope) + Asia.

Europe (continent west of *Asia*)
Name is very old: mentioned in Greek hymn to Apollo written in 6th century BC. Originally name applied only to part of *Balkan* Peninsula: north *Greece*, *Albania* and *Macedonia*. Name originated in Near East, from Assyrian ereb = 'darkness, west', ie 'land of the setting sun' (compare *Asia*).

Eureka (port in north-west *California*, USA)
Named by first settler, James Ryan, who on landing here in 1850 is said to have exclaimed 'Eureka!' (Greek = 'I have found it'). Not clear whether he meant land or gold.

Everest, Mount (highest mountain in world, in *Himalayas*, on frontier of *Nepal* and *Tibet*)
Named after Sir George Everest (1790–1866), Surveyor General of India, said by some newspapers of the time to have had 'more to do with papers than with mountains'. Tibetan name is Chomolungma = 'mother goddess of the earth'.

Extremadura (historic province in *Spain*)
Of same origin as *Estremadura*.

Eyre, Lake (South *Australia*, north of *Adelaide*)
Named after English explorer Edward J. Eyre (1815–1901), who discovered it in 1840.

87

F **Fairbanks** (town in *Alaska*, USA, north-east of *Anchorage*)
Named in 1902 after C. W. Fairbanks, American politician from *Indiana*, later vice-president of USA.

Falkland Islands (in South *Atlantic*, east of *Magellan Strait*)
Originally Davis Land (discovered by Captain John Davis in 1592), then named Hawkins Maidenland in 1594 by Sir Richard Hawkins in honour of English queen Elizabeth I (the 'Maiden' queen). Finally named by Captain John Strong in 1690 after Viscount Falkland, chief minister of state of Charles I, who had financed Strong's expedition.

Farewell, Cape (1) (in extreme south of *Greenland*)
Point of departure of English explorer John Davis in 1586 on his voyage of discovery to *Canada*.

Farewell, Cape (2) (in extreme north of South Island, *New Zealand*)
Point of departure of Cook in 1770 on his voyage of discovery to east *Australia*.

Faroe Islands (in North *Atlantic*, between *Iceland* and *Shetland Islands*, *Scotland*)
Probably from Danish faar = 'sheep' + öe = 'island'; islands were settled by Norsemen in 861.

Fernando Po (volcanic island in Gulf of *Guinea*, West *Africa*)
Named after Portuguese explorer Fernão do Po, who discovered it in 1741 (though he himself named it Formosa—Portuguese = 'beautiful').

Ferrara (province and its capital in north-east *Italy*)
From Italian ferraria = 'forge, ironworks'. Name was first used in Middle Ages.

Fiji (group of islands in South-West *Pacific*, north of *New Zealand*)
Of uncertain origin. Perhaps derived from native name of main island, Viti, applied by European explorers to whole group.

Finger Lakes (in *New York* state, USA)
So named because of their long, narrow shape.

Finistère (department of west *Brittany, France*)
From Old French = 'end of the earth' (Latin finis terrae), ie promontory, in same sense as Cape *Finisterre* and peninsula Land's End in Cornwall, *England*.

Finisterre, Cape (headland in north-west *Spain*)
From Spanish fin de tierra (Latin finis terrae) = 'end of the earth'. (Compare *Finistère*, for which spelling Finisterre is not correct.)

Finland (republic in north-west *Europe*)
Name is of Swedish origin = 'land of the Finns', whose own name is of uncertain origin: perhaps from Germanic finden = 'to seek', ie 'seekers, nomads'. Finns call their own country Suomi, from word probably = 'lake, swamp': Finland has over 60,000 lakes.

Flanders (historic region in west *Belgium* and north-east *France*)
From Flemish Vlaanderen, probably = 'low-lying marsh'. Not likely to be from Roman division of Franks into Fluminarii = 'river-dwellers' (said to have inhabited modern Flanders) and Ripuarii = 'shore-dwellers'.

Flinders, River (*Queensland, Australia*)
Named after English navigator Matthew Flinders (1774–1814) who explored coasts of *Australia* and also gave his name to Flinders Chase, Island and Range.

Florence (city in central north *Italy*)
In 200 BC Etruscan name was Faesulae or Fiosele, and in 82 BC Roman name was Colonia Florentia = 'flowering colony', either in literal sense ('with many flowers') or in sense of 'flourishing'. Benvenuto Cellini had theory that name was originally Fluentia = 'flowing', as town was on River *Arno*.

Florida (state in south-east USA)
From Spanish Pascua florida = 'flowering Easter'; territory was first

sighted, probably on Palm Sunday but perhaps on Easter Sunday, by Spanish expedition of Ponce de León in 1513. Name could also have had literal sense of 'flowering' (as with *Florence*).

Flushing (seaport in south-west *Netherlands*, at mouth of River *Scheldt*)
English version of name is corruption of Dutch Vlissingen = 'fortress on the water'.

Foggia (city in south-west *Italy*, north-west of *Bari*)
Possibly from Latin foveae = 'pits, cellars' (on the Piano delle Fosse = 'plain of pits'), or from Italian dialect word fosse = 'cisterns, tanks' (used for watering flocks of sheep).

Fontainebleau (town in central north *France*, south-east of *Paris*)
Early name was Fons Bleaudi. First word is Latin = 'fountain'; second ultimately derives from Indoeuropean bla = 'to gush, to spout'. Meaning therefore is 'gushing fountain'. Town is famous for hunting-lodge built here in 998 by French king Louis I and for palace of Francis I which developed from it in 16th century.

Formosa (alternative name of *Taiwan*)
Portuguese = 'beautiful'; name was given to island by Portuguese explorers in 1516.

Fort Lamy (capital of *Chad*, Central *Africa*)
Founded by French colonisers in 1900 and named after French soldier and explorer François Lamy (1858–1900).

Fort Worth (city in *Texas*, USA, west of *Dallas*)
Named after American general William Worth, hero of Mexican War of 1846–8.

France (republic in west *Europe*)
Named after Franks, Germanic people who settled in what was Gaul in 5th century AD, with their own name = 'freemen'.

Franche-Comté (historic province in east *France* near Swiss frontier)
French = 'free county'; region was granted special privileges in 9th century by Emperor Lothaire, son of French king Louis I.

Frankfurt (1. city in West *Germany* on River *Main*; 2. city in East *Germany* on River *Oder*)
The 2nd city took name from 1st, = 'ford of the Franks', ie 'ford where Franks crossed the river'. Name later acquired meaning of 'free ford', in sense of city offering access to south *Germany*. (Franks in fact never inhabited 2nd city. For origin of name of Franks, see *France*.)

Franklin (district of North-West Territories of north *Canada*, in *Arctic*)
Named in memory of English polar explorer and admiral Sir John Franklin (1786–1847), who died in the *Arctic* while searching for the North West Passage. Many places in *Canada* are named after him, including mountains, lakes, islands, strait, cape.

Franz Josef Land (group of islands in *Arctic*, north of *Novaya Zemlya*, USSR)
Discovered by an Austrian-Hungarian expedition led by Julius von Payer and Karl Weyprecht in 1873, and named after Austrian emperor Franz Joseph I (1848–1916).

Frascati (town and resort in central west *Italy*, south-east of *Rome*)
Named after church of St Mary and Sebastian 'in the bushes' (Italian in frascata), built here in 9th century.

Fraser, River (in British *Columbia*, north-west *Canada*)
Named after Scot Simon Fraser who crossed Rocky Mountains in 1806–8 and set up a trading station on Fraser Lake.

Freetown (capital of *Sierra Leone*, West *Africa*)
Founded in 1787 as English settlement for liberated slaves. (Compare *Libreville*.)

Fremantle (city and seaport in Western *Australia*, south-west of *Perth*)
Founded in 1829 by English governor James Stirling, who named it after

91

Captain Freemantle who had made survey here before him and annexed the territory.

Friendly Islands (alternative name for *Tonga*)
Name given in 1773 by Cook for friendly welcome accorded him by natives. Islands had been discovered by Dutch expedition of Cornelius Schouten and Jacob le Maire in 1616 and explored by Tasman in 1643.

Frisian Islands (off west coasts of *Netherlands,* West *Germany* and *Denmark*)
From inhabitants, Frisians, with name probably derived from Old High German fri = 'free' (compare *France*), or possibly from Old Frisian frisiaz = 'frizzled (hair)' or from Indoeuropean fer, fars = 'coast'.

Frunze (capital of republic of *Kirghizia*, USSR)
Founded as fortress in 19th century with name Pishpek. In 1926 renamed Frunze in honour of Russian revolutionary leader M. V. Frunze (1885–1925), who was born here.

Fujiyama (extinct volcano, highest mountain in *Japan*, west of *Tokyo*)
The 1st element is of uncertain meaning; 2nd is Japanese yama = 'mountain'. Name has been variously interpreted as 'mountain of immortality', 'mountain of abundance' and even 'beauty of the long slope hanging in the sky'. The 1st element could perhaps be from Ainu word = 'fire'.

Furneaux Islands (in *Bass Strait* off north-east *Tasmania*, south of *Australia*)
Named after Tobias Furneaux (1735–81), captain of one of Cook's ships, who discovered them on Cook's 2nd expedition of 1772–4.

G **Gabon** (republic in West *Africa*)
Named after River Gabon, whose estuary was discovered by Portuguese explorers in 1485 and named Gabão = '(sailor's) cape', perhaps because of appearance of clothing worn by natives here.

Galapagos Islands (in *Pacific*, on equator west of *Ecuador*, South *America*)
From Spanish galapago = 'tortoise'; Spanish explorers who discovered islands in 1535 were impressed by large numbers of giant tortoises (*Testudo elephantosus*), which have since become almost extinct.

Galicia (1) (historic region in *Carpathians*, modern *Ukraine* and west *Poland*)
Name is Latin form of Old Russian Galich, of uncertain origin; perhaps from Slavonic root gala = 'mountain', or from Lettish and Lithuanian gals = 'end, peak', or from Polish hala = 'mountain pasture'.

Galicia (2) (historic kingdom in north-west *Spain*)
Named after Iberian-Celtic tribe, with their own name from Celtic cala = 'waterway', ie 'dwellers by the water'.

Galilee (sea and region in north *Israel*)
From Hebrew galil = 'district' (ie of Gentiles, not Jews).

Gallipoli (peninsula in north-west *Turkey* on *Dardanelles*, and port here)
From Greek kalliopolis = 'beautiful city'. Turkish name, Gelibolu, is corruption of this.

Gambia (republic in West *Africa*, surrounded by territory of *Senegal*)
Named after River Gambia, in turn named by Portuguese who discovered it in 15th century and who had corrupted native name Ba-Dimma = 'river'.

Gambier Islands (in South *Pacific*, south-east of *Society Islands, Polynesia*)
Discovered in 1797 and named after English admiral Lord James Gambier (1756–1833).

Ganges, River (long river of *India* and *Bangladesh*, flowing into Bay of *Bengal*)
From Sanskrit and modern Hindi ganga = 'river'.

Garda, Lake (in north *Italy*, east of *Milan*)
From lakeside town with name = 'watch-tower, guard-post'. Roman name was Benacus, probably from Latin bi(-n-)aqua = '(place on) two waters', ie situated at point where lake divides into two bays.

Garonne, River (in south-west *France*)
Possibly from pre-Indoeuropean karr = 'rock, stone' + Gaulish onno = 'river'. From Garonne derives name of *Gironde* department.

Gascony (historic province in south-west *France*)
Latin name was Vasconia, from inhabitants Vascs (Basques), who in 6th century were driven out of their territory in south *Pyrenees* by Western Goths and settled here.

Gaza (town in south-west *Palestine*)
From Hebrew azah = 'strong' (ie 'fortress').

Geelong (seaport in *Victoria*, *Australia*, south-west of *Melbourne*)
From aboriginal word = 'swampy plain'.

Geneva (city and lake in *Switzerland*)
From Celtic gena = 'mouth, estuary'. City stands at mouth of River *Rhône*.

Georgetown (capital of *Guyana*, South *America*)
Originally held by Dutch from 1784 to 1812, with name Stabroek = 'standing pool'. When country was annexed in 1812 by British, as British *Guiana*, town was renamed Georgetown in honour of English king George III (reigned 1760–1820).

George Town (official name of *Penang*, north *Malaya*)
Named after English king George IV in whose reign (1820–30) it was founded.

Georgia (1) (state in south-east USA)
Became British colony in 1732 and was named in honour of English king George II (reigned 1727–60).

Georgia (2) (republic in south USSR, south of *Caucasus*)
Ancient name (BC) of west part of territory was Colchis, and later Iberia.
Eastern people were known as Gurz or Gurdzh, of unknown meaning,
and this gave Russian name Gruzia, anglicised as Georgia.

Germany (country of Central *Europe*, politically divided into East and
West since 1945)
Named after Germans, people whose name spread BC to other peoples
and later to whole family Germanic) of languages. Roman name for
territory between River *Rh(ine* and River *Danube* was Germania, after
inhabitants, whose own name has many possible origins, eg german =
'greedy hands', ermana = 'big (strong) hands'. German name of country
is Deutschland, from Old High German thiuda = 'people' + land =
'country'. French name, Allemagne, is from tribe Alemanni (Alamanni),
with name = 'all men'.

Gettysburg (small town in south *Pennsylvania*, USA, south-west of
Harrisburg)
Named after James Gettys, who planned the town + German burg =
'town'. Famous as site of Battle of Gettysburg (1863).

Ghana (republic in West *Africa*)
Before 1957 was *Gold Coast*; then took name of former Negro country
which existed here in 4th–13th centuries but covering much larger territory (corresponding to that of modern *Mauritania* and west *Mali*).

Ghats (mountain ranges of *India*—Eastern Ghats and Western Ghats—
running parallel with coast)
From Sanskrit word = 'passes'. In Hindustani also = 'landing stairs' (with
reference to those at *Benares* on River *Ganges*).

Ghent (city in east *Flanders*, *Belgium*)
Probably from Celtic condati = 'confluence'; town is situated at point
where River *Scheldt* flows into River Lys.

Gibraltar (rocky mountain and British colony at its foot in extreme south
of *Spain*)

From Arabic Jebel-al-Tarik = 'mountain of Tarik' (Arab general Tarik ibn Zaid who crossed to territory from *Africa* in 711 and captured it).

Gilbert Islands (in South-West *Pacific*, north-east of *New Guinea*)
Discovered by Cook and named after Joseph Gilbert, captain of one of his ships, the *Resolution*, who explored them in 1788.

Gippsland (district in south-east *Victoria, Australia*)
Named by Polish explorer Count Strzelecki in 1840 after Sir George Gipps, Governor of *New South Wales.*

Gironde (department in south-west *France*, forming estuary of River *Garonne* and River *Dordogne*)
Name is variant of *Garonne*, of same origin.

Goa (territory on west coast of *India*)
Probably corruption of Portuguese Goe moat = 'fruitful land'; territory was Portuguese province from 1510 to 1961.

Gobi (desert in Central *Asia*, largely in *Mongolia* and north *China*)
From Mongolian kobi = 'desert', though Mongolians have no name for whole desert but only for sections of it. Chinese name is Shamo = 'sandy sea'.

Godwin-Austen, Mount (2nd highest mountain in world, in *Karakoram* range, north *Kashmir, India*)
Named after Lieutenant-Colonel Godwin-Austen of Survey of India, who first sighted it in 1865. Alternative name is *K2.*

Gold Coast (former name of *Ghana*)
Name was given by Portuguese in 1471, with reference to gold found as natural deposit here in rivers. Name changed to *Ghana* in 1957.

Golden Gate (strait at entrance to *San Francisco* Bay, *California*, USA)
So named by Drake in 1578 when he found *California* to be a gold-bearing region. Therefore has sense of 'gate to the land of gold'.

Golden Horn (inlet of *Bosporus* forming harbour of *Istanbul, Turkey*)
So named because of abundance of fish, especially tunny, which are
trapped here on entering bay from *Black Sea*. 'Golden' refers to 'richness'
of fish; 'Horn' to shape of harbour, which is branched and winding like
antlers.

Good Hope, Cape of (headland in south-west *Cape Province*, South
Africa)
First rounded by Portuguese navigator Bartholomew Diáz in 1488, who
named it Cabo Tormentoso = 'stormy cape' (it is here that waters of
Atlantic and Indian Ocean meet). But Portuguese king John II regarded
such a harsh name unpromising for possible future trade with *India* and
renamed it Cabo da Bõa Esperança = 'cape of good hope'.

Gorky (city and port on River *Volga*, east of *Moscow*, USSR)
So named in 1932 in honour of Russian writer Maxim Gorky, born here
in 1868. Earlier name was Nizhny Novgorod = 'lower Novgorod' (ie
situated 'lower'—further south—in country than *Novgorod* in north-west
USSR).

Gotland (island in *Baltic Sea*, off south-east coast of *Sweden*)
Possibly from Germanic word = 'god' (island was centre of heathen cult),
or from word = 'water current'. More likely to be derived from name
of Goths, who inhabited Sweden early AD, with their own name probably
deriving from Old Norse gotnar = 'men'.

Graham Land (peninsula in *Antarctic*, west of *Weddell Sea*)
Discovered by John Biscoe in 1832, who named it after Sir James Graham,
First Lord of Admiralty.

Grahamstown (town in *Cape Province*, South *Africa*, north-east of *Port
Elizabeth*)
Named after Scottish colonel John Graham, who founded it in 1812.

Granada (province and city in *Andalusia*, south *Spain*)
Said to be from Spanish = 'pomegranate', not because many grow here,
but because town is situated on 4 hills divided like the divisions of a

pomegranate. Or possibly from Arabic kurn = 'hill' + nattah = 'stranger' (ie 'hill of strangers').

Gran Chaco (large plain in South *America*, largely in north *Argentina* and south *Paraguay*)
From Spanish gran = 'big' + Indian (Guarani) chaco = 'hunting field'.

Great Barrier Reef (greatest coral reef in world, off north-east coast of *Queensland*, *Australia*)
So named by Cook in 1770. Reefs and islands form great natural break-water (barrier) stretching nearly 1,200 miles (2,300km).

Great Bear Lake (in *Mackenzie*, North-West Territories, *Canada*)
Probably translation of Indian name (through French Lac du grand ours), given to lake perhaps to commemorate killing here of unusually large bear.

Great Britain (kingdom of *England*, *Scotland* and *Wales*, west *Europe*)
'Great' as opposed to 'Little' Britain, ie *Brittany*.

Great Slave Lake (in south *Mackenzie*, North-West Territories, *Canada*)
Named after Indian tribes who once inhabited its shores and were driven north by Cree Indians who called them Awokanak = 'slaves'.

Greece (republic in south-east *Europe*)
Name is of Italic origin; Greeks were small tribe living in Aipiros (region in modern north-west *Greece* and south *Albania*), nearest part of *Balkan* Peninsula to *Italy*. Name then spread to whole country. Name of people probably derives from Indoeuropean gra = 'venerable'.

Greenland (large island belonging to *Denmark* off north-east coast of North *America*)
Name is of Scandinavian origin and is literal = 'green land'. Given by Norseman Eric the Red in 982 with aim of attracting settlers here, though country is in fact largely cold and infertile.

Grenada (one of *Windward Islands, West Indies*)
Discovered by Columbus in 1498 who named it after Spanish town *Granada*.

Grenoble (city in south-east *France*)
Latin name was Gratianopolis = 'town of Gratian' (Roman emperor who founded it in 4th century). Modern name derives from this.

Guadalquivir, River (river of south *Spain* flowing south-west through *Seville* into *Atlantic*)
From Arabic Wad-al-kebir = 'river of great water'. (Guada- is common 1st element of many Spanish names, from Arabic wadi = 'river, ravine'.)

Guadeloupe (one of *Windward Islands, West Indies*)
Discovered by Columbus in 1493 who named it Santa Maria de Guadelupe after monastery on River Guadelupe in *Estremadura*, west *Spain*.

Guam (largest of *Marian Islands*, West *Pacific*)
First sighted by Spanish explorers led by Magellan on St John's Day 1521 and named San Juan (= 'St John'). Present name is native corruption of this.

Guatemala (republic in north of South *America*)
Name is Spanish version of Indian (probably Tuendal) uhatzmalha = 'mountain that gushes out water' (referring to volcano Agua), though earlier explanation of origin had been from Aztec quauhtemellan = 'land of the eagle' (tribal totemic bird).

Guernsey (2nd largest of Channel Islands, west of *Normandy, France*)
Possibly from Old Norse gron(-s-)oy = 'green island', or perhaps from Breton guern = 'alder-tree'. Roman name may have been Sarnia or perhaps Lisia.

Guiana (name of various countries in north-east of South *America*: 1. British Guiana (now *Guyana*); 2. Dutch Guiana (now Surinam); 3. French Guiana)
Discovered by Columbus in 1498 and explored in 1499 by Vespucci and

Hojeda, latter naming territory after people, the Guaizas, whose own name = 'respected' (ie 'we who must be respected').

Guinea (1. republic in West *Africa*; 2. Equatorial Guinea, Spanish territory on Gulf of Guinea, West *Africa*; 3. Portuguese Guinea, overseas territory in West *Africa*)
Probably from Berber aguinau = 'black (-skinned people)'.

Gulf Stream (warm ocean current in North *Atlantic*)
Originates in Gulf of *Mexico*; name was suggested in 1772 by American statesman Benjamin Franklin. Earlier name was *Florida* Stream.

Guyana (republic in north-west of South *America*)
Same word as *Guiana*; until 1966 was British *Guiana*.

Guyenne (historic province in south-west *France*)
Corruption of Latin Aquitania (French *Aquitaine*); in 12th century province consisted of duchy formed from *Aquitaine* and *Gascony*. (Name also spelt Guienne.)

H **Haarlem** (city in north *Netherlands*, west of *Amsterdam*)
From Dutch haar = 'height' + lem = 'clay'.

Hague, The (city—seat of government but not capital—in west *Netherlands*)
Originally hunting-lodge of Dutch counts, set in a wood, from Dutch gravenhage = 'count's enclosure' (Old High German hagan = 'hedge').

Haifa (chief seaport of *Israel*, on *Mediterranean* north-east of *Tel Aviv*)
Probably from Hebrew keph = 'cliff'.

Haiti (republic in west part of island of *Hispaniola*, *West Indies*)
From native (Caribbean) name, probably = 'mountainous', or perhaps 'rocky, high'.

Halifax (city and seaport in *Nova Scotia*, east *Canada*)
Founded by English settlers in 1749 and named in honour of Earl of Halifax (1661–1715), who as President of Board of Trade had actively supported British colonisation.

Hamburg (city in north of West *Germany*, at mouth of River *Elbe*)
From Germanic ham = 'inlet' + burg = '(fortified) town'. Or perhaps from Hammaburg = 'fortress in a wood'. City was founded by Charlemagne in 811.

Hamilton (1) (city in *Ontario*, *Canada*)
Founded in 1813 by George Hamilton, who had bought farmland here the previous year.

Hamilton (2) (city in state of *Ohio*, USA)
Named in honour of Alexander Hamilton (1757–1804), American statesman and officer in War of Independence. Various other American towns are also named after him.

Hamilton (3) (city on North Island, *New Zealand*)
Named after English captain John Hamilton, killed here in 1864 in war against Maoris.

Hanoi (capital of North *Vietnam*)
Original name was Kecho = 'capital'. Present name came into use only at turn of century, = 'surrounded by a river' (ie by *Red River*).

Hanover (city and former province in central West *Germany*)
Original name was Honovere = 'high bank' (ie built on banks of navigable River Leine).

Harpers Ferry (small town in West *Virginia*, USA)
Named after Robert Harper, who started ferry service here about 1748. Town lies at confluence of River *Potomac* and River Shenandoah.

Harrisburg (state capital of *Pennsylvania*, USA)
Named after English Quaker John Harris, whose son founded city in 1785, + German burg = 'town'.

Hartford (state capital of *Connecticut*, USA)
Originally named Newtown when founded by English settlers in 1635; renamed Hartford in 1637 after English town Hertford (but spelt with 'a' to reflect pronunciation).

Harz Mountains (range in West *Germany* between River *Elbe* and River *Weser*)
From Old High German hart = 'wood, forest' (not from modern German Harz = 'resin'). Mountains are well wooded and were once 90% covered with trees.

Havana (capital of *Cuba*)
Of unknown origin, perhaps from Indian tribal name. Founded in 1514 by Spanish explorer Diego Velasquez with name San Cristobal de la Habana (= 'St Christopher of Habana') in honour of Christopher Columbus.

Hawaii (group of islands in North *Pacific*, a state of USA)
Discovered by Spanish explorers in 1527 and given native (Polynesian) name = 'place of the gods', referring to two volcanoes Mauna Kea and Mauna Loa, regarded as abode of the gods. In 1778 Cook (murdered here the following year) named them *Sandwich Islands*. Name reverted to Hawaii in 1898.

Hawkes Bay (province on North Island, *New Zealand*)
Named in 1769 by Cook after Admiral Sir Edward Hawke, First Lord of British Admiralty. Name originally given to bay, after which province was named.

Hebrides (group of islands off west coast of *Scotland, Great Britain*)
Of unknown origin; mentioned by Pliny as Hebudae and by Ptolemy as Edoudai. Norsemen named them sudur öer = 'southern islands' (ie in

relation to *Norway*); 1st element of this name is preserved in name of bishopric of Sodor and Man, which formerly included Hebrides.

Heidelberg (city in West *Germany*, south-east of *Mannheim*)
Probably from German Heidelbeere = 'bilberry', or possibly from Heid = 'heath' + Berg = 'mountain'.

Helena (state capital of *Montana*, USA)
Named after home town Helena, *Minnesota*, of one of gold-seekers here in 1864, when town was founded.

Heligoland (island in *North Sea* off north-west coast of West *Germany*)
From Old High German heilag = 'holy' + land; there was once a heathen shrine on the island. But could also perhaps be from Old Friesian halik = 'steep' (island has steep cliffs) + land.

Helsinki (capital of *Finland*)
Founded by Swedes in 1550 with name Helsingfors, from name of tribe, Helsingi, + Swedish fors = 'waterfall' (of River Wanda, near which town was built). In 1648 town was moved to present site on Gulf of *Finland*. Helsinki is Finnish version of Swedish name.

Hercegovina (with *Bosnia* forms north republic of *Yugoslavia*)
From Serbian = 'duke land' (from Old High German herizoge = 'duke'); country became dukedom (duchy) in 1448 and kept name while under Turkish rule from 1483 to 1878.

Hessen ('Land' in west of West *Germany*, former grand duchy)
Probably from name of Germanic tribe Hatti who inhabited central *Germany* early AD. Their name comes from Germanic hattu = 'hat', with reference to Turkish-style turbans that they wore. In 8th century name became Hessii, then Hessia.

Himalayas (mountain system in Central *Asia*, largely in south *Tibet*)
Probably from Sanskrit hima = 'snow' + alaya = 'abode', although another explanation gives derivation of name from goddess Shimalia (= 'mistress of the white mountain').

Hispaniola (island in *West Indies*, divided into (west) *Haiti* and (east) *Dominican Republic*)
Discovered by Columbus in 1492 who named it Española (Spanish = 'Spanish'), although native name of whole island then was *Haiti*. This was later corrupted to Hispaniola.

Hobart (capital of *Tasmania, Australia*)
Until 1881 was Hobarttown; named after English Secretary of State Lord Hobart who founded city in 1804 and used island as penal colony.

Hohenzollern (ancestral castle of Hohenzollern dynasty on Zollernberg Mountain, south-west of *Stuttgart*, West *Germany*)
From German hoch = 'high' + 1st element of name of Mount Zollern, from Old German zolra = 'sugar-loaf mountain' (ultimately from Indo-european tul = 'mountain, height'). Name Hohenzollern (that of Swabian family which became successively Electors of *Brandenburg* (1415–1701), kings of *Prussia* (1701–1918) and German emperors (1871–1918)) combined with that of *Württemberg* to form 'Land' of Württemberg-Hohenzollern in 1945. (See also *Baden-Württemberg*.)

Hokkaido (north island of *Japan*)
Japanese = 'northern land'. Before 1868 was Yezo or Jesso.

Holland (used as alternative name for *Netherlands*, but properly name of two provinces: North Holland and South Holland)
Possibly from Dutch holt = 'grove' + land, ie 'wooded land'; or perhaps from hal = 'low' + land, with same meaning as *Netherlands*.

Honduras (republic in Central *America*, with *Belize*, formerly British Honduras to the north of it)
From Spanish = 'depths'; story is that when Spanish sailors reached coast of Honduras in 1524 they thanked God for having brought them safely over the depths of the *Atlantic*; sea off the coast here is in fact very deep and for many years a good harbour could not be built.

Hongkong (British crown colony on coast of south *China*, chiefly an island)
From Chinese Hiangkiang = 'favourable water', 'good harbour'.

Honolulu (state capital of *Hawaii*, USA)
From Hawaiian hono = 'harbour' + lulu = 'quiet, calm'.

Honshu (largest of islands forming *Japan*)
Japanese = 'chief island'.

Hook of Holland (seaport in south *Netherlands*, west of *Rotterdam*)
From Dutch hoek = 'point, edge'; port is at south-west extremity of province of South *Holland*.

Horn, Cape (rocky headland in extreme south of South *America*)
First rounded in 1616 by Dutch navigator Schouten, who named it after his native town in the *Netherlands*, Hoorn (in province of North *Holland*).

Houston (city in state of *Texas*, USA)
Founded in 1836 and named after General Samuel Houston (1793–1863), who gained independence of *Texas* from *Mexico*.

Hudson Bay (gulf in north *Canada*)
Named after English explorer Henry Hudson (1550–1611), who discovered it in 1610. The previous year he had explored Hudson River, which he had named North River.

Humboldt, River (in state of *Nevada*, USA)
Named after German scientist Alexander von Humboldt (1769–1859), who had explored North *America* in 1799–1804. After him are also named Humboldt Bay (*California*), Humboldt Sea, Humboldt Mountains.

Hungary (republic in south-east of Central *Europe*)
Possibly from name of people, Ugrians, who originally lived on River Ugra, in basin of River *Danube*. Hungarians call themselves Magyars, from kär = 'man' + prefix ma = 'land', ie 'landsmen, natives'.

Huron, Lake (one of Great Lakes, between USA and *Canada*)
From name of Indian Huron tribe who once lived on its shores. French settlers named them thus from their bristly hair, which was like that of a boar (French hure = 'boar's head'), perhaps also with reference to their 'bristly' nature.

Hwang-ho, River (2nd longest river in *China*, also known as *Yellow River*)
Chinese = 'yellow river'.

Hyderabad (city in central south *India*)
From Persian name Haidar, through Arabic, + Iranian abad = 'town', ie 'Haidar's town'. (Personal name = 'lion', regarded as ruler's title.)

I

Ibadan (capital of west state of *Nigeria*, West *Africa*)
From Arabic ibada = 'divine service'; city has long been a centre of Islam.

Iberia (ancient name for peninsula of *Portugal* and *Spain*)
From name of River *Ebro*, formerly Ebros, which flows through it. (See *Ebro, River*.)

Ibiza (one of *Balearic Islands* in *Mediterranean*, off east coast of *Spain*)
Name is Phoenician, given by Carthaginians when they settled on these islands in 654 BC. Probably from Phoenician word = 'island', or perhaps connected with Basque ibis = 'stream'. Could also be from Phoenician ibrusim = 'island of fir trees'.

Iceland (island republic in North *Atlantic*)
Name is literal = 'ice land'. Given, in form Island, by Viking Floki who landed on island in 960s, although another Viking had landed on opposite coast nearly 100 years before him and had given island name of Snjoland = 'snow land'.

Idaho (state in central east USA)
An Indian (Kiowa-Apache) name of uncertain meaning: possibly = 'fish-

eaters' or 'mountain gem' (referring to deposits of gold and silver in mountains).

Île de France (historic region in north *France* with *Paris* as centre)
French = 'island of France', either because region is watered by many important rivers (eg *Marne*, *Seine*, *Oise*) or because it was administrative centre from which early French kings ruled.

Illinois (state in central east USA)
Named after River Illinois (tributary of *Mississippi*), in turn named after Indian Illini tribe, with name derived from Algonquian word = 'people, men, warriors'. Final 's', indicating plural, was added by French settlers who conquered territory in 1673.

India (republic in South *Asia*)
Named after River *Indus*, which flows through it. (India is one of few countries to be named after a river.)

Indiana (state in central east USA)
Latin-type name was given by French settlers in 1702 after Indian tribes who formed population of territory, and was officially adopted about 1765 by land developers here known as the Indiana Company. State was formed in 1816, though by 1830s not one native Indian was left.

Indianapolis (state capital of *Indiana*, USA)
Name was given to city when it was founded in 1820, from Indiana + Greek polis = 'town'.

Indonesia (republic of South-East *Asia*)
From name of *India* + Greek nesos = 'island', ie 'island India'.

Indus, River (great river of *India* and *Pakistan*, flowing into Arabian Sea)
From Sanskrit sindhu = 'river'. Romans and Greeks left off initial 's' when pronouncing name.

Innsbruck (city in west *Austria*)
From German Brücke = 'bridge' + name of River Inn, on which
city stands. Name of river is probably from Celtic enos = 'water'.

Interlaken (resort in *Alps, Switzerland*)
From Latin inter = 'between' + lacus = 'lake'. Town is situated between
Lake Thun and Lake Brienz. Name is of Latin origin, not Germanic, as
town arose by Augustinian monastery in 1130.

Ionian Sea (part of *Mediterranean* between south *Italy* and *Greece*)
Named after Greek people, Ionians, who settled on most of islands in
Aegean Sea, with their own name = 'wanderers, rovers'.

Iowa (state in central USA)
Named in 1846 after River Iowa, tributary of *Mississippi*. Name is of
Indian (probably Sioux) origin, possibly = 'cradling', or from tribal name
Ayuba = 'sleepy' (nickname given to tribe, in sense 'sleepy', by neigh-
bouring Dakotas). French map of 1673 records name in form Ouaouia-
tonon.

Iran (kingdom in South-West *Asia*)
From Sanskrit aria (Iranian ariya) = 'worthy', name originally applied to
Indoeuropean people who had settled here several thousand years BC
and from whom Iranian family of languages originated. Name of country
until 1935 was *Persia*.

Iraq (republic in South-West *Asia*)
From Arabic = 'shore, lowland'. Country lies in basin of River *Tigris*
and River *Euphrates*.

Ireland (republic west of *Great Britain*)
Name is in English form = 'land of the Irish'. Irish name of country is
Eire, from Old Irish eirin (compare poetic name Erin) = 'western' or
possibly 'green' (compare name Emerald Isle, used in poetic or familiar
sense).

Irrawaddy, River (main river of *Burma*, flowing south-west through entire length of country)
From Sanskrit airawati = 'water-possessing current'. (Connection with Arabic wadi = 'river, ravine' is unlikely.) Folklore derives name from mythical elephant of Indra, the sun god.

Irtysh, River (rises in *China* and flows west through USSR to join River *Ob*)
Perhaps from Mongolian ertis = 'river', or from Kazakh ir = 'land' + tysh = 'to dig' (though name existed before Kazakhs settled upper reaches of river). Also perhaps from Bashkir yrtysh = 'rushing' (though river is largely slow-flowing). Most likely is connected with Turkish ir = 'to flow'.

Islamabad (capital of *Pakistan*)
Iranian = 'city of Islam' (Islam + Iranian abad = 'city').

Ismailia (city on *Suez* Canal, *Egypt*)
Named after Ismail pacha, Turkish khedive (viceroy) of *Egypt* from 1863 to 1879. Under his rule *Suez* Canal was completed (1869).

Israel (republic in South-West *Asia*)
From name of Hebrew tribe, Israelites, in turn with name derived from Israel = 'god Isra'. In 10th century BC was name of Jewish country in *Palestine*. In Bible Israel is 2nd name of Jacob and is interpreted as 'God's warrior' (with reference to Genesis 32:28), from Hebrew sara = 'to fight' + El = 'God'.

Istanbul (city in *Turkey*, on *Bosporus*)
Many possible meanings; among them are: 1. from Turkish islam-bul = 'city of Islam'; 2. from Greek eis ten polis (dialect is tan polin) = 'into the city'; 3. (most likely) from Turkish corruption of *Constantinople*, its name to 1930.

Istria (peninsula in north-west *Yugoslavia*, near Italian frontier)
From Latin name Histria = 'land of the Istrians' (Illyrian tribe warring against *Rome* in 3rd century BC). Greek writers saw connection between

Istria and their name for River *Danube*—Istros—but this link is not clear.

Italy (republic in south *Europe*)
Name arose about 500 BC as Vitalia and originally applied only to *Calabria*, where the Vitali, tribe from the north, had settled, with their own name taken to be connected with Latin vitulus, Greek italos = 'calf', but this may merely be attempt to explain unknown word. In 2nd–1st centuries BC name gradually spread and with rise of Roman empire was established to apply to whole *Apennine* Peninsula.

Ithaca (one of islands in *Ionian Sea*, off west coast of *Greece*)
Letter 'i' which begins many *Mediterranean* names derives from Phoenician word = 'island, land'. Original name was Thiaki, of uncertain meaning. (Ancient Ithaca in *Odyssey* was not this island but Levkas. When name 'transferred' is not clear.)

Ivory Coast (republic on Gulf of *Guinea*, West *Africa*)
Ivory (elephant tusks) was traded here by Portuguese from 1447, later in keen competition with the East India Company.

J

Jackson (state capital of *Mississippi*, USA)
Named after Andrew Jackson (1767–1845), 7th president of the USA. (Named after him also is Jacksonville, *Florida*.)

Jaffa (seaport in *Israel*, on *Mediterranean*)
From Arabic yafe = 'bright, visible' (ie visible from afar). In 1949 incorporated with *Tel Aviv*.

Jakarta (capital of *Indonesia*, on north-west coast of *Java*)
Perhaps from Sanskrit jaya-kerta = 'place of victory', or from Iranian kert = 'built (place)'. Dutch settlers who built fort here in 1619 called it Batavia, after their homeland on delta of River *Rhine*, but city reverted to name Jakarta in 1949.

Jamaica (island in *Caribbean Sea*, south of *Cuba*)
From native (Arawak) name Xaymaca = 'island of springs', with reference to plentiful supply of water on island. Columbus, who landed on island in 1494 named it Santiago as landing was made on St James's Day (Spanish San Jago), 25 July, but native name was one that was adopted.

Jamestown (town in *New York* state, USA)
Named after James Prendergast, an early settler (unlike Jamestown, *Virginia*, named in 1607 in honour of English king James I).

Jan Mayen (island in *Arctic* between *Iceland* and *Spitzbergen*)
First discovered by Hudson (see *Hudson Bay*) in 1607; rediscovered by Dutch captain Jan Mayen in 1611 and named after him.

Japan (country in East *Asia*)
From Chinese name of country Ji-pen-kue = 'land of the rising sun'. Japanese name of country is Nippon, from ni = 'sun' + pon = 'country'.

Java (island in *Indonesia*, south-east of *Sumatra*)
From Sanskrit java dvipa = 'barley island'. Settlers here BC from *India* and *Ceylon* found rich barley fields on island.

Jefferson City (state capital of *Missouri*, USA)
Named after Thomas Jefferson (1743–1826), 3rd president of the USA.

Jericho (village in *Jordan*, north-east of *Jerusalem*)
From Hebrew j'richo = 'scented place' (with Hebrew addition ir hall' marim = 'of the palm-trees').

Jersey (largest of Channel Islands, west of *Normandy*, *France*)
Possibly from Old Frisian gers = 'grass' + Scandinavian ey = 'island', or from personal name of Viking who seized the island—Geirr—or from Old Norse jarl = 'lord' (compare English word 'earl'). Unlikely that name is a corruption of Roman Caesarea (after Julius Caesar) since it has not been finally proved that this name applied specifically to Jersey (though it did to some island between *Orkney* and *Ushant*).

Jerusalem (city in *Palestine*, since 1948 politically divided between *Israel* and *Jordan* but since 1967 recognised as capital of *Israel*)
In Assyrian cuneiform was Urusalimmi, and in Egyptian hieroglyphics Shalam. Probably from Old Hebrew shalem = 'peace' (derived from root word = 'stone') + ieru = 'house, people', ie 'house of peace' or 'house of stone'.

Jodhpur (city in north-west *India*, south-west of *Delhi*)
From Sanskrit = 'military town'.

Johannesburg (city in *Transvaal*, South *Africa*)
Founded by gold-seekers in 1886. Probably named after Johannes Rissik, government surveyor of *Transvaal* + Dutch burg = 'town', or possibly after Johannes Meyer, mining commissioner of the time.

Jordan (kingdom in South-West *Asia*)
Named after River Jordan, with its own name of unknown origin: perhaps from Hebrew jarden = 'drain, channel' or jarda = 'to rush, to roar'.

Juan de Fuca Strait (separates *Vancouver* Island, *Canada*, from state of *Washington*, north-west USA)
Discovered in 1592 by Greek sailor Apostolos Valerianos, serving *Spain* with name of Juan de Fuca, and named after him.

Juneau (state capital of *Alaska*, USA)
Named in 1881 after Joseph Juneau, one of first gold-seekers here the previous year.

Jungfrau (mountain in Swiss *Alps*, south-east of *Interlaken*)
German = 'maiden', either because silhouette of mountain has appearance of nun or girl in white or, more likely, so named in contrast to neighbouring dark Mönch (= 'monk') Mountain.

Jura (mountains on frontier between *France* and *Switzerland*, and French department here)
From Gaulish juris = 'wooded height'.

Jutland (peninsula in north *Europe* consisting of south *Denmark* and north of West *Germany*)
Named after Jutes, Germanic tribe who settled here BC, with their own name derived from Old Norse jotar, ytar = 'people'.

K2 (alternative name of Mount *Godwin-Austen*)
So named from initial of *Karakoram* range, in which it was the 2nd to be measured. (It is also the 2nd highest in the world.)

Kabalega Falls (at north end of Lake *Albert* on River *Nile*, *Uganda*, Central *Africa*)
So named in 1972 after former king of Bunyoro, *Uganda*, who fought against British. Earlier name was *Murchison Falls*.

Kabul (capital of *Afghanistan*)
On River Kabul, with name of uncertain origin: perhaps from Iranian word = 'storehouse' (unlikely, as town was named after river), or from similar word = 'red' or 'horse'.

Kalahari (desert chiefly in *Botswana*, South *Africa*)
From native name Karri-karri = 'torture, suffering'. Element -ri is regarded as Bechuana (Tswana) variant of Hottentot -di. Boers (Dutch colonisers of South *Africa*) called it Bosjeveld = 'thorn field', from which Bushmen (aboriginal race of South African hunters) derive their name.

Kalgoorlie (town in Western *Australia*, north-east of *Perth*)
From aboriginal name of native shrub.

Kamchatka Peninsula (in north-east USSR, between Sea of *Okhotsk* and *Bering Sea*)
Originally name of river. Various explanations of name, all equally unlikely: eg from name of brave warrior Khonchat, from mythical lovers Kam (son of a mountain) and Chatka (daughter of a volcano) who threw themselves to their death here, from local name of Khonchalo tribe, from dialect word = 'cape, peninsula'.

H

Kampala (capital of *Uganda*)
Possibly from Bantu word = 'antelope' or 'basket'; explanation of origin
of these not known.

Kanchenjunga (3rd highest mountain in world, in *Himalayas*, on *Nepal-
Sikkim* border)
Said to be from Tibetan kang = 'snow' + chen = 'big' + dzo = 'treasure'
+ yoga = 'five', ie '(mountain of) five big snowy treasures' (referring to
its 5 peaks).

Kandy (town in *Sri Lanka*, north-east of *Colombo*)
From Sinhalese kandi = 'mountain' (ie 'town in mountain country').

Kansas (state in central USA).
Named after River Kansas, in turn named after Indian (Sioux) tribe—
although perhaps tribe was named after river. Tribal name said to mean
'south wind', ie tribe living where south wind blows. Final 's' is probably
plural, added by French settlers (compare *Arkansas*).

Karachi (city and seaport on Arabian Sea in *Pakistan*, of which it is
former capital)
In 18th century was only small fishing village. Name derives from Baluchi
tribe of Kulachi (see *Baluchistan*).

Karakoram Range (mountain system in north *Kashmir*, Central *Asia*)
From Turkish kara = 'black' + korum = 'mountain, rocks'.

Karlovy Vary (resort and spa in *Czechoslovakia*, north-west of *Prague*)
Czech = 'Charles's springs'. German emperor Charles (Karl) IV (1316–
78) discovered warm mineral springs here in 1347 when building a
hunting-lodge. German name is Karlsbad, with same meaning.

Karlsruhe (city in West *Germany*, north-west of *Stuttgart*)
German = 'Charles's rest'. German count Karl Wilhelm von Baden-
Durlach built a hunting-lodge here in 1715, thus founding present city.

Kashmir (state in north-west *India*)
Said to be from Sanskrit Kasyapa-mira = 'sea of Kasyapa' (legendary hero who, according to story, cut pass through mountains here to link up mountain lake with River *Indus*).

Kassel (city in West *Germany*, north-east of *Frankfurt*)
From Latin castellum = 'castle'. Name in 913 was Chasalla. (Castle was that of Roman fortress.)

Katanga (province in south-east *Zaire*, Central *Africa*)
From African (Hausa) name = 'walls, buildings', referring to former capital, Yoruba. In 1972 renamed Shabu, Swahili = 'copper'.

Katmandu (capital of *Nepal*)
Perhaps = 'border place', or named after ancient temple of Kastamandap (= 'wooden temple').

Kattegat (strait between *Sweden* and *Jutland, Denmark*)
From Old Scandinavian kati = 'ship, vessel' + gata = 'way'. Old Dutch maps name it as *Skagerrak*, and *Skagerrak* as Nordzee (= 'north sea').

Kazakhstan (republic in south USSR, in Central *Asia*)
Named after Kazakhs + Iranian stan = 'country'. Kazakhs, people of Turkish origin, have name probably = 'freemen'.

Keeling Islands (alternative name for *Cocos Islands*, Indian Ocean)
Discovered in 1609 by Captain William Keeling of East India Company.

Keewatin (east district of North-West Territories, *Canada*)
From Indian (Cree) word = 'north wind', ie tribe living where north wind blows. (Compare *Kansas*.)

Kennedy, Cape (on east coast of *Florida*, USA)
Formerly *Cape Canaveral*. Renamed in 1963 in honour of John F. Kennedy (1917–63), 35th president of the USA.

Kentucky (state in central south USA)
Named after River Kentucky, in turn with name derived either from Indian kan-tuk-kee = 'land dark with blood' (referring to inter-tribal wars), or from kan-tuc-kec = 'land of green reeds', or, most likely, from Iroquois ken-take = 'plain, meadow-land'.

Kenya (republic in East *Africa*)
Named after Mount Kenya, with name of uncertain origin: possibly simply Swahili = 'mountain'.

Kerguelen Island (in Indian Ocean, south-east of South *Africa*)
Named after French navigator Yves Joseph de Kerguelen (1734–97), who discovered it in 1772.

Kermadec Islands (in South-West *Pacific*, north-east of *Auckland*, *New Zealand*)
Named after French navigator Huon Kermadec who, with D'Entrecasteaux and Raoul, explored them in 1793. They were discovered by English captain Sever in 1788.

Khartoum (capital of *Sudan*)
Headland between River White *Nile* and River Blue *Nile*, where city was founded in 1822; was called in Arabic Ras-el-hartum = 'end of the elephant trunk' (referring to its outline).

Khmer Republic (official name since 1970 of *Cambodia*)
Named after native population, Khmers, whose name is of uncertain meaning, but known to be very old. Originally, final 'r' was not pronounced. Name *Cambodia* is Portuguese corruption of Khmer name Kamnuchia.

Kicking Horse Pass (through Rocky Mountains, on frontier between *Alberta* and British *Columbia*, *Canada*)
Discovered in 1859 by Sir James Hector, English geologist, who was kicked by his horse while making his way through it.

Kiel (city in *Schleswig-Holstein*, in north of West *Germany*)
In 10th century was thom Kyle (modern German zum Kiele = 'on the keel'), related to Norwegian kel = 'narrow bay, inlet'.

Kiev (capital of republic of *Ukraine*, USSR)
Probably named after legendary ferryman Kiy, said to have founded city on River *Dnieper*; or perhaps after Prince Kiy, who came with Oleg to capture the city in the 9th century. Kiev is the most ancient of all Russian cities: Ptolemy mentions city called Metropolis on River *Dnieper* in 2nd century AD, and it is known as the 'mother of Russian cities'. Exact year when founded not known.

Kilimanjaro (extinct volcano in north-east *Tanzania*, East *Africa*)
From Swahili kilima = 'mountain' + njaro = 'god of cold'.

Kimberley (1. district in north of Western *Australia*; 2. town in *Cape Province*, South *Africa*)
Both named after English colonial secretary Lord Kimberley.

Kingston (capital of *Jamaica*, *West Indies*)
Founded in 1693 on site of earlier Port Royal, which was destroyed by earthquake in 1692 and named in honour of English king William III.

Kinshasa (capital of *Zaire*, Central *Africa*)
From Bantu word of unknown origin. Name was that of African settlement where Sir H. M. Stanley founded *Léopoldville* in 1882; in 1966 name reverted to Kinshasa.

Kirghizia (republic in south-east USSR, bordering on *China*)
Named after its native inhabitants, Kirghiz, with their own name of Mongolian origin, perhaps from kir = 'plain' + kis = 'to wander', but this could be attempt to explain unknown name.

Kishinev (capital of republic of *Moldavia*, USSR)
Possibly from Moldavian neu = 'new' + Turkish kishlah = 'winter quarters'.

Klondike, River (in *Yukon* Territory, north-west *Canada*)
From Indian throndik = 'river of fish'. River gave its name to gold-bearing region here (see *Dawson*).

Klyuchevskaya (highest active volcano in *Asia*, on *Kamchatka* Peninsula, USSR)
Named after nearby town of Klyuchi, in turn with name derived from Russian = 'springs'.

Knoxville (city in east *Tennessee*, USA)
Founded in 1786 and named in honour of American general Henry Knox (1750–1806), hero of War of Independence.

Komandorskiye Islands (between *Kamchatka* Peninsula and *Aleutian Islands*, east USSR)
Discovered in 1744 by expedition led by Commodore (Russian komandor) Bering, after whom are named one island of this group—Bering Island—and *Bering Strait*.

Korea (peninsula in East *Asia* on which are situated two politically divided republics of North Korea and South Korea)
No satisfactory explanation for name. Korean name is Choson which, as well as Japanese name for peninsula—Chosen—is said to derive from Chinese = 'country of morning coolness'.

Kosciusko, Mount (highest mountain in *Australia*, in *New South Wales*, south-west of *Canberra*)
Named after Polish hero and statesman Tadeusz Kosciuszko (1746–1817) by Polish explorer Strzelecki, who discovered it in 1839.

Krakatoa (volcanic island in Sunda Strait, between *Java* and *Sumatra*)
Native name is Kerakatau, from Javanese rekatak = 'to split, to crack' + prefix ke-. Volcano erupted violently in 1883, blowing entire north part of island away.

Krakow (3rd largest city in *Poland*, on River *Vistula*, south-west of *Warsaw*)

From personal name Krak or Krok (founder of city or lord of castle here), whose name is of uncertain origin, possibly from a Celtic word or from Slavonic krak = 'raven'.

Kuala Lumpur (capital of *Malaysia*)
From Malay kuala = 'mouth, estuary' + lumpur = 'mud'. City is situated at mouth of River Klang.

Kuril Islands (chain of islands extending from south end of *Kamchatka* Peninsula, USSR, to *Hokkaido, Japan*)
Number of possible explanations: 1. from Ainu kuri = 'cloud, mist'; 2. from Russian kurit = 'to smoke' (referring to steam from volcanoes on islands); 3. from Ainu kur = 'people' (as name of inhabitants). Japanese name is Chisima = 'thousand islands'.

Kuwait (Arab state and its capital on north-west coast of Persian Gulf)
Arabic name is El Kuwait = 'the enclosed', possibly referring to Portuguese fort built here in 16th century.

Kwangchow (city in south-east *China* on River *Canton*)
From Chinese kwan = 'broad, large' + chow, denoting town of upper rank, ie 'capital of a large territory' (province of Kwangtung). Former name of Kwangchow was *Canton*.

Labrador (coastal territory in north-east *Canada*)
Many theories concerning origin of name: 1. sighted by Portuguese navigator Gaspar de Cortereal in 1501 and named by him Terra de lavradores = 'land of ploughmen' (he saw natives as potential slaves working on plantations); 2. (less likely) named by Spanish or Portuguese explorers after Terre de Labour, a small territory in south France; 3. (least likely) from French le bras d'or = 'the golden arm', name given by optimistic gold-seekers. Originally settled by Norsemen in 10th century with name Hellaland = 'rocky land'; later named Vinland = 'land of grapes'.

Laccadive Islands (in Arabian Sea, west of coast of *Malabar*, south-west *India*)
From Sanskrit lakshna = 'a hundred thousand' + dvipa = 'island' (there are in fact 14 coral islands and several reefs; perhaps name was meant to include *Maldives* as well).

Ladoga, Lake (largest lake in *Europe*, in north-west USSR, north-west of *Leningrad*)
Probably from Finnish aalto = 'wave' or ala = 'lower'.

Ladysmith (town in *Natal*, South *Africa*, north-west of *Durban*)
Named in honour of (Spanish) wife of Sir Harry Smith, British Governor of Cape Colony 1847–52. Nearby town of Harrismith bears his own name.

Lafayette (cities in *Indiana* and *Louisiana*, USA)
Named in honour of French soldier and statesman, Marquis de la Fayette (1757–1834), who in 1776 fought against British in American War of Independence.

Lagos (capital of *Nigeria*)
Name given by Portuguese in 16th century from lagoon (Portuguese lagos) surrounding island on which city stands.

Lahore (2nd largest city of *Pakistan*, north-east of *Karachi*)
Said to have been founded by Lo (Sanskrit Lava), son of Hindu god Rama, but this is merely attempt to explain earlier name of unknown meaning.

Lampedusa (island in *Mediterranean* between *Malta* and *Tunisia*)
From Italian lampada = 'lamp', referring to its lighthouse.

Landes (region in south-west *France* extending parallel to Bay of *Biscay*)
French = 'heathland, sandy waste', from Gaulish landa (related to English word 'land'). Region consists largely of moorland and sand-dunes.

Languedoc (region and historic province in southern *France*)
Name arose at end of 13th century, from French langue d'oc = 'language
of oc': oc was French word for 'yes' in south of country, as distinct from
oil (later oui) in north.

Lansing (state capital of *Michigan*, USA)
Named by emigrants from village of Lansing in *New York* state, in turn
named after John Lansing (1754–1829?), politician and lawyer.

Laos (kingdom of South-East *Asia*, between *Thailand* and *Vietnam*)
Named after Thai people Lao (from Lava), with plural 's' added by
Portuguese settlers.

La Paz (capital of *Bolivia*, South *America*)
Full name, given by Spanish in 1548 to mark peace concluded between
two warring factions, was Pueblo Nuevo de Nuestra Señora de la Paz =
'new town of Our Lady of Peace'.

Lapland (region in north *Europe* covering north of *Norway*, *Sweden*,
Finland and extreme north-west USSR)
Named after principal inhabitants, Lapps, whose own name derives from
Finnish lappalainen = 'border dwellers'.

La Plata (city on estuary of River *Plate*, *Argentina*, South *America*)
From Spanish name of river—Rio de la Plata (see *Argentina*).

Laptev Sea (part of *Arctic* Ocean, in north central *Siberia*, USSR)
Named in 1913 by Russian Geographical Society in honour of *Arctic*
expedition of 1733–41 made by Lieutenants Dmitry and Khariton Laptev.
Earlier name was Nordenskjöld Sea, after Swedish explorer Nils Nordenskjöld (1832–1901) who discovered North East Passage in 1878–
9.

Las Palmas (largest city in *Canary Islands*, *Spain*)
Spanish = 'the palm-trees' (which are prolific here).

Las Vegas (city in south-east *Nevada*, USA)
Spanish = 'the meadows' (referring to fields used as camp-sites on early trails).

Latin America (term used for *Mexico*, Central *America* and South *America*)
Comprises countries in which are spoken languages derived from Latin—Spanish and Portuguese—as opposed to North *America*, where chief language is English.

Latvia (republic in north-west USSR on *Baltic Sea*)
Named after principal inhabitants, Letts, whose name is of uncertain origin.

Lausanne (city on north shore of Lake *Geneva*, *Switzerland*)
Original name was Lausonna or Leusonna, probably from Gaulish leusa = 'smooth stone'. Other theories trace name back to Celtic personal name Lousis or to Roman name of Celtic origin Lausodunum = 'fort on the river Laus' (with name of river = 'stony').

Lebanon (republic in South-West *Asia*, south of *Syria*, on *Mediterranean*)
Named after mountains, in Hebrew l'banon = 'white mountain', referring either to snow or to colour of limestone rock.

Leeuwin, Cape (headland in extreme south-west of Western *Australia*)
Named after Dutch ship, with name = 'lioness', whose crew discovered it in 1622.

Leeward Islands (in *West Indies*, extending south-east from *Puerto Rico* to *Windward Islands*)
Islands are situated in position sheltered from prevailing north-east Trade Winds (in contrast to *Windward Islands*).

Leghorn (city and seaport in north-west *Italy*, south-west of *Pisa*)
English name is corruption of Italian Livorno, named after Liburni, ancient inhabitants of modern *Croatia*. Element -orn seems to have been

added by Illyrians. Town was once Portus Herculis = 'port of Hercules' (Greek god venerated along *Mediterranean* coast).

Le Havre (city and seaport in north *France* at mouth of River *Seine*)
Founded by French king Francis I in 1517 as Le Havre de Grâce = 'the harbour of grace', as was on site of fishing village with chapel dedicated to Notre Dame de Grâce (Our Lady of Grace).

Leiden (city in south *Netherlands*, north-east of The *Hague*)
Probably from leithen = 'canal' (city is on canal leading to *North Sea*), or from Gaulish Lugdunum (see *Lyons*).

Leipzig (city in East *Germany*, south-west of *Berlin*)
From Slavonic name Lipsk, from lipa = 'lime-tree'. In 920 town was fishing village by lime-grove.

Le Mans (city in north-west central *France*, south-west of *Paris*)
Roman name in 2nd century BC was Vindinon, from Gaulish vindo = 'white'. In 4th century AD took name of tribe of Cenomanni (perhaps = 'hill dwellers'), whose capital city it was. Name was shortened to Celmans, with 1st element confused with French le = 'the'. (See also *Maine* (2), *Cremona*.)

Lemnos (island in north of *Aegean Sea*, between *Greece* and *Turkey*)
From Phoenician = 'white': sailors were impressed by hills of white pumice-stone.

Lena, River (longest river in USSR, rising near Lake *Baikal* and flowing north-east into *Arctic* Ocean)
From Evenki (Tungus) name Yelyuyone, probably = 'river'.

Leningrad (2nd largest city in USSR, in north-west of Gulf of *Finland*)
Named in 1924 after Russian revolutionary leader V. I. Lenin (1870–1924) + Slavonic grad = 'town'. From 1914 to 1924 was *Petrograd*, and before 1914, from founding in 1703, *St Petersburg*.

León (province and its capital and historic kingdom in north-west *Spain*)
From Latin legio = 'legion': town was station of Roman 7th legion.

Léopoldville (former name of *Kinshasa, Zaire*)
Founded by English explorer Sir H. M. Stanley in 1882 and named in
honour of Belgian king Léopold II (1835–1909), who financed his ex-
plorations, + French ville = 'town'. In 1966 renamed *Kinshasa*.

Lesbos (island in *Aegean Sea* off west coast of *Turkey*, belonging to
Greece)
From Greek = 'wooded'.

Lesotho (kingdom in South *Africa*)
Named after principal inhabitants, Suto tribes, as was name of country
before 1966, *Basutoland*.

Levant (name for coastal countries of east *Mediterranean*, usually extending from *Greece* to *Egypt*)
From Italian levante = 'rising', ie lands in east, where sun rises.

Lexington (town in *Kentucky*, USA, south-east of *Louisville*)
Name ultimately derives from English village of Laxton, Nottingham-
shire (once Lexin(g)ton), but was influenced by title of Lord Lexington
(1661–1723) and brought to *Kentucky* in 1776 by hunters who had heard
news of battle of Lexington in *Massachusetts* the previous year.

Liberia (republic in West *Africa*)
From Latin liber = 'free'; Liberia was established in 1822 as territory for
liberated American Negro slaves.

Libreville (capital of *Gabon*, Central *Africa*)
From French libre = 'free' + ville = 'town'; town was founded in 1848
for freed slaves (compare *Liberia, Freetown*).

Libya (republic in North *Africa*)
Name is very ancient, and was known in Egyptian hieroglyphics of
2000 BC. As yet meaning is unexplained.

Lido (resort just south-east of *Venice, Italy*)
Italian = 'shore' (from Latin litus).

Liechtenstein (principality in Central *Europe*, between *Switzerland* and *Austria*)
Named after princes who founded it in 1719, their own family name deriving from town of Lichtenstein, near *Vienna* (in turn from German lichten = 'to shine, to lighten' + Stein = 'stone', referring to light colour of buildings).

Liège (city and province in east *Belgium*)
Name in 770 was Leodicum, from personal name (Leudi) of lord of castle here. Not likely to be connected with Indoeuropean leod = 'of the people'.

Liguria (region in north-west *Italy*)
Named after Ligures, tribe who inhabited this region BC (on north coast of Ligurian Sea).

Lille (city in extreme north-east of *France*)
From Old French l'isle = 'the island'; city was built as a fortress surrounded by marshes.

Lima (capital of *Peru*, South *America*)
Founded in 1535 by Spanish explorer Francisco Pizarro who named it Ciudad de los Reyes = 'city of the kings' (town was founded on 6 January, Feast of Epiphany). With time, however, city acquired name derived from that of River Rimac (named after god with name = 'he who speaks'), on which it stands.

Limburg (province in east of south *Netherlands*)
First recorded in 1093 with name Lintburch = 'town of lime-trees'.

Limerick (county and town in south-west *Ireland*)
English version of Irish Luimneach, from luimne, diminutive of lom = 'bare, poor', referring to barren earth.

Limoges (city in central *France*, west of *Clermont-Ferrand*)
Name derives from Gaulish tribe Lemovices (who also gave their name
to Limousin), with their own name perhaps = 'dwellers among the elm-
trees'. Earlier name was Augustoritum, from name of Roman emperor
Augustus + Gaulish rito = 'ford'.

Limpopo, River (in South *Africa*, rising in *Transvaal* and flowing
through *Mozambique* into Indian Ocean)
Of uncertain origin. Perhaps = 'crocodile river', its alternative name.

Lincoln (state capital of *Nebraska*, USA)
Named in honour of Abraham Lincoln (1809–65), 16th president of the
USA.

Lions, Gulf of (bay of *Mediterranean* extending from (west) French–
Spanish frontier to (east) *Toulon*)
Not connected with city of *Lyons*, but with lions, either because of statues
of lions set up along coast here or, more likely, because of roaring of sea
when mistral blows (compare *Sierra Leone*).

Lisbon (capital of *Portugal*)
Name is probably of Phoenician origin, perhaps from ippo = 'fence' or
alis ubbo = 'joyful bay'. Not named after legendary hero Ulysses (Odysseus) said to have founded it. Roman name was Olisippo.

Lithuania (republic in north-west USSR on *Baltic Sea*, bordering on
Poland)
Probably from Lithuanian lieti = 'to flow', ie 'land on flowing water'
(*Baltic Sea*), or perhaps from Lithuanian lytus = 'rain'.

Little Rock (state capital of *Arkansas*, USA)
From smaller of two rocks on banks of River Arkansas, named La Petite
Roche (= 'the little rock') in 1722 by French explorer Bernard de la
Harpe.

Lofoten Islands (off north-west coast of *Norway*)
Original meaning lost. Supposed derivation from lo = 'fox' + fot = 'foot' is only attempt to explain unknown name.

Loire, River (longest river in *France*, flowing north-west from central *France* into Bay of *Biscay*)
Roman name was Liger, from Indoeuropean lig = 'to flow, to run'.

Lombardy (region in north *Italy*, bordering on *Switzerland*)
From Germanic tribe of Langobards who settled here in 569. Their own name may = 'long beards' or 'long axes'.

London (capital of *Great Britain*)
Many possible explanations; some are: 1. from Celtic llwyn = 'wood' + dinas = 'town'; 2. from Celtic lon = 'hill' + dun = 'place'; 3. from Celtic llyn = 'water' + dun = 'place'; 4. from Celtic lhong = 'ship' + dinas = 'town, port'; 5. from Celtic londo = 'wild (people)'; 6. from tribal name Londinos.

Londonderry (county and town in north-west of Northern *Ireland*)
Original name was Derry, from Irish doire = 'oak-wood'. Name Londonderry was given in 1612 when city was granted to company of merchants from *London*.

Long Island (in *New York* state, USA)
Name was originally given in 1614 by Dutch settlers. Island is 118 miles (190km) in length.

Lorraine (historic province in north-east *France*)
From Latin Lotharii regnum = 'kingdom of Lothair'; in 843 empire of Charlemagne was divided by his grandsons: central territory (Francia media) went to one of them, Lothair I (795–855), who in turn partitioned it between his sons, the younger, Lothair II (reigned 855–69), receiving the north region, then extending west of River *Rhine* from *North Sea* to the *Alps*, and corresponding to modern Lorraine.

Los Angeles (3rd largest city in USA, in southern *California*)
Full name given by Spanish missionaries, when they settled here in 1781, was El pueblo de Nuestra Señora la Reina de los Angeles de la Porciúncula = 'the city of Our Lady of the Angels of the Little Portion' (the Porciúncula is Franciscan shrine near Assisi, *Italy*). Name was originally given on 2 August 1769 (without first 3 words) to river by which expedition camped, previous day having been Feast of the Porciúncula. Name eventually contracted to Los Angeles (for similar contraction compare *Buenos Aires*).

Louisiana (state in south USA, on Gulf of *Mexico*)
Region was explored by French in 1677–82 and in 1681 was named in honour of French king Louis XIV. Name originally covered much wider territory than today.

Louisville (city in north *Kentucky*, USA)
Founded by French in 1778; in 1780 named in honour of French king Louis XVI, in recognition of his support during American War of Independence.

Loyalty Islands (in South-West *Pacific*, east of *New Caledonia*)
Two islands of group, Lifou and Ouvea, were discovered by French admiral Dumont d'Urville in 1827 and named by him Îles Loyauté with reference to trustworthiness of natives and friendliness of their welcome.

Lübeck (city and seaport in *Schleswig-Holstein*, north of West *Germany*)
Probably from personal name of Slavonic prince Liuba + Slavonic suffix –ichi = 'descendants'. Name was later interpreted to mean 'little stream', from Old German lützel-bek, but this is unlikely derivation.

Lucerne, Lake (central *Switzerland*)
Named after town of Lucerne on its shore; name has several possible origins: 1. from Latin lucerna = 'lighthouse'; 2. from Latin lucius = 'pike-basket' (ie place where pike are plentiful); 3. from Romansch lozzerina = 'marshy place'; 4. after monastery of St Leodegar, founded nearby about 740. German name of Lake is Vierwaldstätter See =

'lake of the four forest cantons' (ie Uri, Schwyz, Unterwalden and Luzern, which surround it).

Lucknow (city in north-east *India*, south-east of *Delhi*)
From Lakhnau = 'town with a good future'.

Lugano, Lake (partly in *Switzerland*, partly in *Italy*)
From Gaulish Lakvannos = 'lake dwellers' (laku = 'lake'), name of people who once inhabited this region.

Lundy (small island in Bristol Channel, south-west *England*)
From Old Norse lundi = 'puffin'—bird for which island is famous.

Lushun (port in north-east *China*)
From Chinese lü = 'army' + shun = 'safely'. English name was *Port Arthur*. Later joined with *Talien* to form new city of *Lü-ta*.

Lü-ta (city and seaport in north-east *China*, on *Yellow Sea*)
From 1st elements of *Lushun* and *Talien*, which merged after World War II to form one city.

Luxembourg (grand duchy and its capital in west *Europe*, bounded by West *Germany*, *France* and *Belgium*)
In 963 name was Lucilinburhuc, from Old Saxon luttil = 'little' + burug = 'town'. Duchy is named after town.

Lvov (city in republic of *Ukraine*, USSR, south-west of *Kiev*)
From personal name Lev (Leo), probably that of Galician prince who built fortress here in 13th century.

Lyons (3rd largest city in *France*, in central south-east, on River *Rhône*)
Roman name was Lugdunum, possibly from Gaulish dun = 'fortress', with 1st element lugus = 'little', or perhaps from name of pagan Celtic god Lug or from Celtic lucodunos = 'bright mountain'. Town was founded in 43 BC.

I

M   **Maastricht** (town in east *Belgium*, north-east of *Liège*)
From Latin trajectum ad Mosam = 'crossing over (river) Maas (*Meuse*)'.

Macao (Portuguese province in south-east *China*, west of *Hong Kong*)
Name is Portuguese corruption (via Amagoa, Amacoa) of Chinese name
Aomin, from Chinese ngao = 'bay' + men = 'gate'. Or perhaps derives
from Chinese Ama-ngao = 'bay of Ama' (goddess worshipped by sailors).

Macedonia (south republic of *Yugoslavia*; historic region on *Balkan*
Peninsula)
Named after Macedonians, Slavonic people who settled here in 6th century AD, though earlier inhabitants had same name, perhaps from Greek
makednos = 'tall, slender'. Or possibly from Old Illyrian maketia =
'cattle'. True meaning uncertain, hence attempt to explain name by story
of legendary king Macedo, son of Zeus, said to have reigned here.

Mackenzie (west district of North-West Territories, north *Canada*)
Named after River Mackenzie, in turn named after British explorer Sir
Alexander Mackenzie (1764–1820) who sailed up it in 1789 on his way to
Arctic Ocean.

McKinley, Mount (in central *Alaska*, highest in USA)
Named in 1896 after William McKinley (1843–1901), 25th president in
the USA.

Madagascar (island republic in Indian Ocean, off South-East *Africa*)
Name before 1960 of *Malagasy Republic*, of which it is a corrupted form.
Originally applied to territory in African mainland, and given by Marco
Polo at end of 13th century (as Madeigascar).

Madeira (group of islands in North *Atlantic* off North-West *Africa*, and
chief island of this group)
Islands have been 'discovered' 3 times by Europeans: 1. by Romans who
called them Insulae purpurrinae = 'islands of purple dye' (got from trees
here), though Carthaginian name was Al Agnam = 'small animals' (ie
goats); 2. by Italian sailors, who took Carthaginian name as Italian leg-

name = 'timber'; 3. by Portuguese in 1420 who translated Italian word into Portuguese, with same meaning, this giving modern name Madeira.

Madison (state capital of *Wisconsin*, USA)
Named in honour of James Madison (1751–1836), 4th president of the USA.

Madras (state and its capital in south-east *India*)
Various unlikely explanations of name, eg from Mandradsh = 'country of Mand' (a god) or 'country of fools', but most likely from Arabic madrasa = 'school' (ie of Moslems).

Madrid (capital of *Spain* and central province of country)
Arabic name was Medshrid, related to matria = 'wood for building, timber': region had abundant wood supply which Arabs used for building.

Magdeburg (city in East *Germany* on River *Elbe*, south-west of *Berlin*)
Name possibly derives from woman's name Magda (ie 'Magda's town'), but uncertain if she owned town or was venerated here. Or perhaps from Celtic pagan god Mogon. More likely derived not from personal name Magda but from German Magd = 'maid', referring to some pagan goddess.

Magellan Strait (in south *Chile*, between mainland of South *America* and *Tierra del Fuego*)
Discovered in 1520 by Portuguese explorer in Spanish service, Fernando Magellan (Fernão de Magelhães).

Maggiore, Lake (in *Lombardy*, north *Italy*, with north end in *Switzerland*)
Italian = 'greater (lake)': lake is longer and wider than neighbouring Lake *Como* and Lake *Lugano*.

Mahé (largest island of *Seychelles*, Indian Ocean)
So named in 1742 by French captain L. Picault in honour of governor of

French possessions in India Mahé de la Bourdonnais. (In Tibetan Mahé = 'buffalo'.)

Main, River (in West *Germany* flowing west through *Frankfurt* to join River *Rhine* near *Mainz*)
From Celtic or Illyrian name Moinas, perhaps derived from Celtic mo = 'slow' + enos = 'water', or from Indoeuropean moinia = 'marsh'. Could also be connected with Celtic magos = 'big'.

Maine (1) (state in *New England*, north-east USA)
Two possible explanations: 1. named by French settlers in 1635 after their native province of Maine—see *Maine* (2); 2. named by English settlers in 1607 with sense of 'mainland' or even 'open sea', to distinguish territory from offshore islands. But French name came after English and may have been attempt to interpret it. Also, English name could be connected similarly with French province Maine since English queen Henrietta, wife of Charles I, had claim to it.

Maine (2) (historic province in north-west *France*, south of *Normandy*)
Ancient name was Cenomania, from Celtic cenn = 'hill', giving name of tribe Cenomanni (= 'hill-dwellers'). Last element gives present name. (Compare *Le Mans, Cremona*.)

Mainz (city in west of West *Germany* on River *Rhine*, south-west of *Frankfurt*)
City is situated at confluence of River *Rhine* and River *Main*. Gaulish name was Moguntiacon, possibly from pagan god Mogon or some personal name (compare *Magdeburg*). Connection with River *Main* not proved.

Majorca (largest of *Balearic Islands*, in west *Mediterranean*)
Roman name was Majorica (insula) = 'greater (island)', ie in relation to *Minorca*. Spanish name, Mallorca, is variant of this.

Malabar (coastal region in south-west *India*)
From Sanskrit = 'mountain country' (Sanskrit malai = 'mountain'; compare *Malaya*). But possibly from Iranian bar = 'shore' (as in *Zanzibar*).

Malacca (state and its capital in south-west *Malaya*)
Probably from Sanskrit maha = 'big' + lanka = 'island'. In fact 'island' is a peninsula.

Málaga (province and its capital in south *Spain*)
Name is of Phoenician origin, perhaps = 'service, business', or less likely from malh, malahah = 'salt place' (ie place where fish are salted).

Malagasy Republic (official name since 1960 of *Madagascar*)
From inhabitants, Malagasy, with name of uncertain meaning, though perhaps connected with name of *Malaya*.

Malawi (republic in Central *Africa*)
From African (Chichewa) word = 'flames', after name of ancient Negro people, Maravi. Meaning probably refers to reflection of rising sun on Lake Malawi and on 3 smaller lakes in country.

Malaya (state forming part of *Malaysia*, peninsula in South-east *Asia* south of *Thailand*)
Probably from Sanskrit malai = 'mountain'.

Malaysia (group of islands in South-East *Asia*, consisting of peninsula of *Malaya* and *Borneo*)
Probably, as *Malaya*, from Sanskrit malai = 'mountain', but perhaps more closely linked to name of *Malacca*.

Maldive Islands (in Indian Ocean, south-west of *Sri Lanka*)
Many possible meanings. Probably from Sanskrit dwipa = 'island' or malai = 'mountain' (or both) or from Malabar maldiva = 'thousand islands' (there are in fact nearly 2,000).

Mali (republic in West *Africa*, south of *Algeria*)
Until 1960 was French *Sudan*, when reverted to Negro name of Mali, applied in 11th–15th centuries to much wider territory. May derive from Mandingo mali = 'hippopotamus'.

Mallorca (Spanish name, also used in English, for *Majorca*)

Malmö (city and seaport in south *Sweden*)
From Old Scandinavian malm = 'sandy land, sandy valley' + oe = 'island'.

Malta (island in *Mediterranean*, south of *Sicily*)
Greek name was Melite, from Phoenician = 'shelter, refuge' (ie from sea). Latin name Melita has been confused with Greek melita = 'honey'.

Man, Isle of (in Irish Sea between north *England* and Northern *Ireland*)
In ancient times was Monapia or Mona, probably from Celtic mennin = 'middle', in sense of island being halfway between *England* and *Ireland*, or possibly from Celtic men = 'rock'.

Manchuria (region in north-east *China*)
Named after inhabitants, Manchus, whose own name derives from Chinese man-chen = 'inhabitant'.

Mandalay (2nd largest city in *Burma*, north of *Rangoon*)
From Sanskrit mandala = 'circle', in sense of holy precinct. Mandalay is great centre of Buddhism.

Manhattan (island in *New York* state, USA)
From Indian (Algonquian) word probably = 'hilly island'. Two (colourful) theories are that name derives from: 1. ma-na-hac-te-neid = 'place of drunkenness', referring to incident in 1609 in which Henry Hudson (see *Hudson Bay*) liberally regaled Indian delegation with spirits on board his ship here; or from 2. (Iroquois) man-hei-tanana = 'place where we were cheated', referring to purchase of Manhattan from Indians in 1610 by Dutch settlers for absurdly low sum of 60 guilders.

Manila (city in *Philippines*, of which it is former capital)
Probably from Tagalog may = 'to be' + nila = 'indigo', ie 'place where there is indigo'.

Manitoba (province in central east *Canada*)
Province is named after Lake Manitoba, in turn named after island in lake with Indian name Manatuapa = 'great spirit' (worshipped here by

Cree tribe, who regarded island as spirit's abode). Or perhaps from Sioux mine = 'water' + toba = 'prairie'. French explorers who discovered lake in 1738 named it Lac des Prairies, as if translating Indian name.

Mannheim (city on River *Rhine* in West *Germany*)
Possibly from personal name Mano + German Heim = 'abode, home'. Or perhaps from older form am-aha-heim = 'dwelling by the river'. The 1st element may be connected with Celtic man = 'boundary stone' (as in Breton word menhir = 'long stone').

Mantua (town in *Lombardy*, north *Italy*, south-west of *Verona*)
Founded in 325, with name probably from Etruscan god Mantus.

Maracaibo (lake and city in north-west *Venezuela*, South *America*)
Name given to town in 1499 by Spanish explorer Alfonso de Hojeda after lake, in turn named after local Indian chief (cacique).

Marathon (village in south-east *Greece*, north-east of *Athens*)
Greek = 'fennel', which once grew in abundance here.

Marches, the (region in central east *Italy* bordering on *Adriatic Sea*)
From Italian marche = 'borderland' (ie of *Ancona*, its capital).

Marian Islands (in West *Pacific*, north of *New Guinea* and west of *Philippines*)
Discovered by Portuguese explorer Magellan in 1521 who called them Islas de los Ladrones, Spanish = 'islands of thieves'. In 1668 islands were renamed in honour of Maria of Austria, wife of Spanish king Philip IV.

Marmara, Sea of (in north-west *Turkey*, between *Black Sea* and *Aegean Sea*)
Named after Island of Marmara in Sea of Marmara, with name derived from Greek marmaros = 'marble': island is famous for its white marble used for building palaces of *Istanbul* and other cities.

Marne, River (in north-east *France*, joining River *Seine* just north of *Paris*)

Said to be from Latin matrona = 'mother', in sense of 'mother of the gods'; more likely to be from either Ligurian ma = 'to roar' or possibly Indoeuropean mad = 'to flow down'.

Marquesas Islands (in South *Pacific*, north-east of *Tahiti*, in French *Polynesia*)
Discovered by Spanish expedition in 1595 and named in honour of Spanish viceroy of *Peru*, Marquis (Spanish Marques) de Mendoza.

Marrakesh (2nd largest city in *Morocco*, south of *Casablanca*)
Founded in 1057 with name Marrakush, Berber = 'fortified'. City gave name to *Morocco*.

Marsala (town and seaport in West *Sicily*, south *Italy*)
Name is from Arabic Mars-el-Allah = 'harbour of Allah'. Arabs founded town in 9th century on ruins of Greek Lilybaion = '(cape) overlooking Libya'.

Marseilles (2nd largest city in *France*, seaport on south coast)
Earliest known form of name is Massalia (Latin Massilia). City was perhaps founded by Phoenicians about 1000 BC and named after tribe Massili, whose own name is of uncertain origin, or more likely by Greeks about 600 BC.

Marshall Islands (in West *Pacific*, east of *Marian Islands*, *Micronesia*)
First sighted by Spanish navigator Alvarez de Saavedra in 1529; explored by English captain J. Marshall in 1788 and named after him.

Martinique (one of *Windward Islands*, *West Indies*)
Discovered in 1502 by Columbus on 15 June, St Martin's Day.

Maryland (state in USA on central East *Atlantic* coast)
Founded by English Baron Baltimore in 1632 and named in honour of Queen Henrietta Maria, wife of King Charles I.

Massachusetts (state in *New England*, north-east USA)
Of uncertain origin; perhaps from Indian (Algonquian) massud-ch-es-et

= 'high hill, little plain', adopted by English from tribal name with 's' added for plural. Name was first given to Massachusetts Bay, then to state with original name Massachusetts Bay Colony.

Mato Grosso (state in central south-west *Brazil*, South *America*)
Portuguese = 'big forest': much of territory is vast tropical rain forest.

Matterhorn (mountain in Swiss *Alps* on Swiss–Italian border)
From German Matte = 'mountain meadow' + Horn = 'peak'. French name is Mont Cervin, Italian is Monte Cervino, both = 'deer mountain (from steep, antler-like peaks).

Mauritania (republic in North-West *Africa*)
From Greek mauros = 'black' (ie black-skinned people); word is from same root as for Moors.

Mauritius (island in Indian Ocean, east of *Madagascar*)
Named by Dutch admiral Van Neck in 1598 in honour of Prince Maurice (Latin Mauritius) of Orange, Stadtholder of United Provinces (modern *Netherlands*).

Mecca (capital of *Saudi Arabia*)
Possibly from Phoenician makak = 'ruined', but more likely from Arabic makorab = 'shrine'; Mecca is holiest city of Islam and birthplace of Mohammed.

Medicine Hat (town in south *Alberta*, *Canada*)
Indian name is Saamis = 'hat of a medicine man'. Name perhaps refers to some incident involving Indian 'medicine man'—possibly inter-tribal battle in which he lost his hat—or to resemblance of nearby hill to a medicine man's hat. Name was given by W. Johnson in 1882.

Medina (town in *Saudi Arabia*, north of *Mecca*)
Full Arabic name is Medinet-an-nabi = 'town of the prophet'; in 622 Mohammed fled here from *Mecca* and died here in 632.

Mediterranean Sea (large sea between *Europe, Africa* and South-West *Asia*)
From Latin Mare mediterraneum = 'sea in the middle of the earth'; Romans regarded it as central sea of Roman empire. Earlier, in 1st century AD, it was Mare nostrum = 'our sea'.

Mekong, River (in South-East *Asia*, on peninsula of Indochina)
Perhaps = 'head of waters' or 'mother of rivers'; 2nd element, kong, probably derives from Sanskrit ganga = 'river' (compare *Ganges*).

Melbourne (capital of *Victoria, Australia*)
Founded in 1835 with name Dutigala; in 1837 renamed Melbourne in honour of English prime minister Lord Melbourne.

Memphis (city in south-west *Tennessee*, USA)
Named in 1826 after ancient Egyptian city of Memphis, partly because name suggested grandeur and wealth of the East, partly, perhaps, because American city had similar position on River *Mississippi* to that of Egyptian city on River *Nile*.

Menorca (Spanish name, also used in English, of *Minorca*)

Menton (town and resort in south-east *France* on *Mediterranean*)
Perhaps from personal Roman name Mento or, more likely, from Celtic men = 'rock'. No connection with French menton = 'chin'.

Mesopotamia (region of South-West *Asia* approximating to modern *Iraq*)
From Greek mesos = 'middle' + potamos = 'river'; much of region is between River *Tigris* and River *Euphrates*.

Messina (city and seaport in east *Sicily*, south *Italy*, and strait between *Italy* and *Sicily*)
Founded in 735 BC by Greek settlers with name of Zankle = 'sickle-shaped', perhaps with reference to curve of headland. In 4th century AD acquired name of Messina, after Greek town of Messana, from which many of emigrants had come. Strait is named after city.

Metz (city in *Lorraine*, east *France*, south of *Luxembourg*)
Roman version of Gaulish name was Divodurum, from diu-dur = 'two rivers'. Later Latin name was Mediomatricum = 'middle of the Matricii' (Gaulish tribe), which was later simplified to Mettis and finally became Metz.

Meuse, River (rises in north-east *France* and flows north through *Ardennes* into *Belgium* and *Netherlands*, then west to join River Waal)
Name, as Dutch version Maas, derives from Celtic Mosa, ultimately connected with Indoeuropean root word mus = 'damp, moisture'.

Mexico (republic in south extremity of North *America* and its capital)
Possibly derived from name of lake which once stood where capital now is, and which was called Metzlianan by Aztecs, from metz-tli = 'moon' (to which lake was dedicated) + atl = 'water'; in 1325 Aztecs founded city on island of this lake, which later came to be called Metz-xih-co = 'in the centre (literally 'navel') of the waters of the moon'. Town gave name to whole territory.

Miami (city and resort in *Florida*, USA)
Probably from Indian (Muskogean) word = 'peninsula dwellers'.

Michigan (state and lake in north USA)
Lake gave name to state; derives from Indian word, perhaps michaw = 'great' + sasigan = 'lake', or perhaps michigan = '(forest) clearing'.

Micronesia (large group of islands in West *Pacific*, north of *Melanesia*)
From Greek micros = 'small' + nesos = 'island', with ending -ia denoting territory. Most of islands in group are small (*Caroline, Marshall, Marian, Gilbert* and others) compared to those of *Melanesia*.

Midway Island (in North *Pacific*, west of *Hawaii*)
Island is situated midway between *America* and *Asia*.

Milan (2nd largest city in *Italy*, in north-west)
In 222 BC was Mediolanum, from Gaulish medio = 'middle' + lan = 'meadow, plain'; town arose in middle of plain of River Olona.

Milwaukee (city in *Wisconsin* and port on Lake *Michigan*, USA)
From name of Indian (Algonquian) tribe once living here, with meaning probably = 'good land'.

Minneapolis (city in *Minnesota*, north USA)
From Minne-, 1st element of *Minnesota*, + Greek polis = 'town'. One of city's parks has Minnehaha Falls, from Indian (Sioux) minnehaha = 'waterfalls' (heroine of Longfellow's *Hiawatha* has this name, with false interpretation of 'laughing water').

Minnesota (state and river in north USA, bordering on *Canada*)
State takes name from river, in turn from Indian (Sioux) minne = 'water' + sota = 'cloudy'.

Minorca (2nd largest of *Balearic Islands*, in west *Mediterranean*)
Roman name was Minorica (insula), from Latin minor = 'lesser' (in relation to *Majorca*). Spanish name of island is Menorca.

Minsk (capital of republic of *Byelorussia*, USSR)
Probably named after some river, though in fact on River Svisloch. There exist Russian Rivers Men, Mena and Menka, whose names can be linked with German River *Main*. Or perhaps from Latvian main = 'marsh'.

Mississippi (state in south USA and longest river, after *Missouri*, in central USA)
From Indian (Algonquian) word = 'great river'; recorded in French text of 1666 as Messipi. River gave name to state when latter was established in 1817. Spanish name for river in 1542 was Soto Rio Grande = 'big river of Soto', after Spanish explorer Ferdinando de Soto who led expedition here in 1539.

Missouri (state and longest river, with *Mississippi*, in USA; in central USA)
From Indian (Algonquian) word = 'muddy' (river carries down much silt). Or perhaps from name of Indian tribe = 'big boat'. State took name from river.

Moldavia (republic in south-west USSR, bordering on *Romania*)
Named after inhabitants, Moldavians, whose own name probably derives
from molid = 'pine', or perhaps from Slavonic mol (Indoeuropean mel)
= 'black' (ie earth).

Mombasa (chief port of *Kenya*, on Indian Ocean)
Probably named after Mombasa, *Oman*; Arab settlement at Mombasa,
Kenya, dates from about 11th century.

Monaco (principality and its capital in south-east *France*, on *Mediterranean*)
From Greek monoikos = 'hermit, monk'; on rock on which city of
Monaco stands there was once (7th–6th centuries BC) a Roman temple to
god Hercules the Hermit (Heracles Monoecus).

Mongolia (republic in east Central *Asia*, formerly called Outer Mongolia)
From inhabitants, Mongols, whose name has basic meaning 'brave ones',
and became established in 13th century as a result of their numerous con-
quests; earlier they had called themselves simply Bide = 'we'.

Monrovia (capital of *Liberia*, West *Africa*)
Named in honour of James Monroe (1758–1831), 5th president of the
USA, in whose term of office it was founded (1822) as a settlement for
liberated American slaves.

Montana (state in north-west USA, bordering on *Canada*)
From Spanish = 'mountainous': Rocky Mountains are in west of state.
Name was originally that of small town of gold-seekers, then of surround-
ing territory, then in 1889 of whole state.

Mont Blanc (highest mountain in *Alps*, in south-east *France*)
French = 'white mountain', with reference to permanently snow-
covered peaks.

*Monte Carlo*

Monte Carlo (resort in *Monaco* on *Mediterranean*)
Italian = 'Mount Charles'; town was founded in 1866 in reign of Monegasque prince Charles III.

Montenegro (republic in south-west *Yugoslavia*, bordering on *Albania*)
From Old Italian = 'black mountain', probably either because mountains are inaccessible and inhospitable or because of their dark colour. Serbo-Croat name, Crna Gora, has same meaning.

Monterrey (city in north-east *Mexico*, Central *America*)
Originally founded as León in 1560, after Spanish town *León*; name changed to Monterrey in 1599 in honour of Gaspar de Zuñiga, Count of Monterrey, Viceroy of New Spain. (American town Monterey on coast of *California* derives from this, with one 'r' reflecting spelling of the time.)

Montevideo (capital of *Uruguay*, South *America*)
Name probably given by Magellan in 1520 to mountain here of which there was a good view, from Portuguese monte vidi eo = 'I saw the mountain' (perhaps a cry from one of the sailors who sighted it). Or possibly from Portuguese map-maker's note on mountain with words monte VI de O = 'sixth mountain from the west', Roman figure VI being read as syllable -vi- and 'O' the Portuguese abbreviation for oeste = 'west'.

Montgomery (state capital of *Alabama*, USA)
Named in 1819 in honour of American general Richard Montgomery, hero of War of Independence.

Montpelier (state capital of *Vermont*, USA)
From name of French city *Montpellier*, as tribute for French support in American War of Independence.

Montpellier (chief city of *Languedoc*, south *France*, north-west of *Marseilles*)
In 975 had Latin name Mons pestellarius = 'woad mountain', probably

142

because was place where this dye was produced. Name eventually contracted to Montpellier.

Montreal (largest city in *Canada*, in south *Quebec*)
Name originally given by French settlers in 1642 was Ville-Marie = 'Marytown' (ie protected by Virgin Mary); later named Montreal = 'royal mountain' (modern French Mont Royal) in honour of French king Francis I who had sent leader of expedition, Jacques Cartier, on colonising mission here. City stands on slope of extinct volcano Mount Royal, so named by Cartier in 1535.

Montreux (town and resort at east end of Lake *Geneva*, *Switzerland*)
From Latin monasterium = 'monastery'; town arose from monastery on island in Lake *Geneva* in 9th century and was then rebuilt on present site in 13th century.

Montserrat (one of *Leeward Islands*, *West Indies*, south of *Antigua*)
Discovered by Columbus in 1493 and named by him probably after monastery of Montserrat (= 'jagged mountain') in *Catalonia*, *Spain*.

Moose Jaw (town in *Saskatchewan*, *Canada*)
First settled in 1882, when named after Moose Jaw Creek. Probably of Indian origin, with meaning on lines of 'place where the white man mended the cart wheel with the jawbone of a moose'.

Moravia (historic region in central *Czechoslovakia*)
Named about 500 BC after River Morava, tributary of River *Danube*. Name of river perhaps derives from Illyrian marus = 'marsh', or Germanic word = 'marshy river'. Or could be connected with Celtic maros = 'great'.

Morocco (kingdom in North-West *Africa*)
Name is Spanish corruption of traditional south capital of *Marrakesh*.

Moscow (capital of USSR)
Named after River Moskva on which it stands. Name of river has many possible origins, among which are: 1. from Slavonic moskva = 'damp,

marshy'; 2. from Slavonic most-kva = 'bridge water'; 3. from Finno-Ugrian moska = 'calf' + va = 'river, water' (ie 'calf ford').

Moselle, River (rises in *Vosges*, and flows north to join River *Rhine* at *Coblenz*)
From Gaulish name Mosella = 'little Mos (Maas)', ie 'a little river like the river Maas (*Meuse*)'.

Mozambique (Portuguese territory in South-east *Africa*)
Portuguese settled on coral island off coast here in 1508; according to records of Vasco da Gama native word mosambuco = 'gathering of boats'. Name then spread to whole territory.

Mukden (alternative name for *Shenyang*, *China*)
From Manchurian = 'height'.

Munich (2nd largest city in West *Germany*, in south)
From Old High German munih = 'monk'; city was built on site of Schäftlarn monastery at Tegernsee.

Münster (city in west of West *Germany*, north of *Dortmund*)
From Old High German munistri, in turn from Latin monasterium = 'monastery'. City has been bishop's seat (see) since 803.

Murchison Falls (former name of *Kabalega Falls*, *Uganda*, East *Africa*)
Named, as are Murchison Rapids on River Shire, south *Malawi*, and River Murchison in Western *Australia*, after British geologist Sir Roderick Murchison (1792–1871). Murchison Falls were renamed in 1972.

Murcia (region and historic kingdom in south-east *Spain*)
Origin uncertain. Name of town here in 3rd century BC, and that of Roman town, unknown.

Murmansk (city and seaport in north-west USSR, on *Barents Sea*)
Built in 1915 as terminus of railway leading to *Arctic Ocean*. Original name was Romanov-na-Murmane (= 'Romanov-on-Murman'), from ruling dynasty of tsars, Romanovs, + Murman, which is not name of

river but of coastal region, perhaps deriving from same root as **Norman** (ie as inhabitants of region were northerners).

Murray, River (chief river of *Australia*, in *New South Wales*)
Named in 1830 by English explorer Charles Sturt after Sir George Murray, English Colonial Secretary. Explanation of name as derived from Gaelic muireach = 'watery land' unlikely.

Nagasaki (city in south-west *Japan*)
Japanese = 'long mountains'; city was founded in 1568.

Nairobi (capital of *Kenya*, East *Africa*)
From Swahili word = 'swamp'; city was founded in 1899.

Namur (province and city in south-west *Belgium*)
In 7th century was Namucum, probably from Celtic nam = 'to bend, to wind' + suffix -uco (perhaps = 'bend of a river'). But could also be from Celtic nan-to = 'valley, meadow', ie 'settlement in a valley', or from nemeto = 'holy wood'. Final letter 'r' is still unexplained.

Nanking (city in east *China*, on River *Yangtse*)
Chinese = 'southern capital', in contrast to northern capital, *Peking*.

Nantes (city in west *France*, on River *Loire*)
From name of Gaulish tribe Namneti, whose capital it was.

Napier (seaport and capital of *Hawkes Bay* province, North Island, *New Zealand*)
Founded in 1856 by English commissioner of crown lands Alfred Domett, who named city after British field-marshal Sir John Napier (1810–90).

Naples (3rd largest city in *Italy*, seaport on *Tyrrhenian Sea*, south-east of *Rome*)
Greek name was Neapolis = 'new town'; town was 'new' in relation to older town of Cumae.

Nashville (state capital of *Tennessee*, USA)
Named in honour of American general Francis Nash (1742–77), hero of War of Independence, + French ville = 'town'.

Nassau (capital of *Bahamas*)
Founded in 1729 with name Charlestown, in honour of English king Charles II; later changed to Nassau when William III, of house of Orange-Nassau, came to throne. (Royal house derived name from former German duchy of Nassau, in turn from Old High German naz = 'damp, marshy' + augia = 'land'.)

Natal (east province of South *Africa*)
Discovered by Portuguese expedition led by Vasco da Gama on Christmas Day (Portuguese Natale) 1497. The 1st English settlement here was called Port Natal, later renamed *Durban*.

Navarra (province in north-east *Spain*)
Name dates back to before 8th century. Probably from Basque nava = 'plain' + arra, word of unknown meaning.

Nazareth (town in north *Israel*, south-east of *Haifa*)
Probably from Old Hebrew natzar = 'to guard' (ie 'defence post'). Not likely to be from Arabic natara = 'to be green'.

Nebraska (state in central USA)
From Indian (Sioux) ni = 'water' + bthaska = 'flat', name given to River Platte, in turn anglicised version of French Rivière Plate, translation of Indian name. State adopted Indian name of river.

Nepal (kingdom in South *Asia*, bordering on north-east *India*)
Possibly from Sanskrit nipalaya = 'abode at the foot' (ie of the *Himalayas*), or from Tibetan niyampal = 'holy land'. Both names imply sanctity of mountains.

Netherlands (kingdom in north-west *Europe*)
Name is literal, ie 'nether (low-lying) lands'. Also known as *Holland*, strictly the name of 2 provinces, North and South, in the country.

Nevada (state in west USA)
Named after *Sierra Nevada*, range of mountains which are in fact not in Nevada, but in neighbouring state of *California*.

Nevis (one of *Leeward Islands, West Indies*)
From original Spanish name Nuestra Señora de las Nieves = 'Our Lady of the snows' (referring to white cloud on peak of mountain giving appearance of snow). Last word was corrupted to Nevis, also used for highest mountain on island. Name probably not given by Columbus, though island was discovered by him in 1493. No connection with Mount Ben Nevis, *Scotland*, in naming, though this mountain has similar origin and meaning (from Gaelic beinn-nimh-bhatais = 'mountain with its peak in the clouds').

Newark (city in *New Jersey* and town in *Ohio*, USA)
Ohio town takes name from one in *New Jersey*, which was given to it in 1666 by English settler and missionary Abraham Pierson (1608-78), from English town of Newark (present Newark-on-Trent). Not likely, in spite of religious background, that name derives from 'new ark'.

New Brunswick (province in east *Canada*, on Gulf of *St Lawrence*)
Separated from *Nova Scotia* in 1784, with name as compliment to English king George III, of house of *Hanover* or *Brunswick*.

New Caledonia (island in South-West *Pacific*, east of *Queensland, Australia*)
Name given by Cook, who discovered it in 1774, after Roman name for *Scotland*, with which, however, neither it nor he has any connection.

New England (name of 6 states in north-east USA: *Maine, New Hampshire, Vermont, Massachusetts, Rhode Island, Connecticut*)
Name was given to territory by English captain John Smith in 1614—appropriately, since 1st English settlement was established 4 years later at Plymouth, *Massachusetts*, by Puritans who had sailed from English town Plymouth in the *Mayflower* (although Smith gave name in general way, on lines of New France and New Spain).

Newfoundland (province in extreme east of *Canada*, consisting of island and *Labrador*)
Discovered by Italian-born English explorer John Cabot in 1497. Territory acquired this obvious name almost immediately (an English text of 1498 refers to 'the new-found land').

New Guinea (island to north of *Australia*, consisting of (west) West Irian and (east) *Papua*)
Discovered by Portuguese explorer Jorge de Menezes in 1526; in 1545 named New Guinea by Portuguese navigator Ortez de Rez because of resemblance of natives to those of *Guinea*, West *Africa*.

New Hampshire (state in *New England*, north-east USA, bordering on *Canada*)
Name given in 1629 by English settler Captain John Mason (1586–1635), to whom King Charles I had granted the territory, after his home county of Hampshire.

New Hebrides (group of islands in South-West *Pacific*, west of *Fiji*)
Discovered by Spanish explorer de Quiros in 1606; in 1774 named New Hebrides by Cook after Scottish islands, with which, however, neither he nor they are connected.

New Jersey (state in east USA, on *Atlantic* coast)
Name given in 1664 by one of proprietors of territory, Sir George Carteret (1610–80), after his native island of *Jersey*, Channel Islands.

New Mexico (state in south-west USA bordering on *Texas* and *Mexico*)
Name first given, as Nuevo Mexico, by Spanish explorer Francesco de Ibarra in 1562, in hope that territory would become as rich as original *Mexico*, lying to the south. In 1848 name was anglicised as New Mexico.

New Orleans (largest city in *Louisiana*, USA)
Founded by French settlers in 1718 and named, as Nouvelle Orléans, in honour of French regent Philippe, Duc d'Orléans (during minority of Louis XV). Name anglicised as New Orleans in 1803.

New South Wales (state in south-east *Australia*)
Discovered by Cook in 1770 and so named by him because of apparent resemblance of coastline to that of south *Wales*. Originally Cook considered name New Wales but rejected it in favour of New South Wales.

New York (state and its capital—New York City, largest city in USA—in north-east USA)
Settled by Dutch in 1624 who named it New Amsterdam; captured by English in 1664 and named New York in honour of Duke of York, to whom colony had been entrusted by his brother, King Charles II.

New Zealand (British dominion in South-West *Pacific*, consisting of two islands, North Island and South Island)
Sighted by Dutch explorer Abel Tasman in 1642 and named by him Staaten Landt = 'land of the States' (ie of the *Netherlands*), but name was changed following year by Dutch authorities to Nieuw Zeeland = 'new sea-land' (with reference also, doubtless, to Dutch province of Zeeland, which consists largely of islands). Name was later anglicised to New Zealand, although 'Zealand' is a word that is neither Dutch nor English.

Niagara (river and falls on frontier of *Canada* and USA between Lake *Erie* and Lake *Ontario*)
Probably from Indian (Huron) word = 'thundering water', but could also be from Iroquois word = 'point of land cut in two' (referring to point where river flows into Lake *Ontario*).

Nicaragua (republic in Central *America*)
Discovered in 1522 by Spanish explorer Gil Gonzalez, who named territory after Indian chief who owned it. Chief's name is of uncertain meaning.

Nice (seaport and resort in south *France*, on *Mediterranean*)
Was Greek colony of Nikaea (Latin Nicaea); city was dedicated to Nike, Greek goddess of victory, and so named to mark victory of Greek settlers from Massilia (modern *Marseilles*) over Ligurians in 3rd century BC.

Nicosia (capital of *Cyprus*)
Named after Nike, Greek goddess of victory (compare *Nice*). Greeks settled island about 800 BC.

Niger (republic in North-West *Africa* and long river flowing south through it and *Nigeria* into Gulf of *Guinea*)
From African (Tuareg) n'eghirren = 'flowing water'. Country is named after river, as is *Nigeria*. Not connected with Latin niger = 'black'.

Nigeria (republic in West *Africa*)
Named after River *Niger*, in whose basin it is situated.

Nijmegen (city in east *Netherlands*, south of *Arnhem*)
In Roman times was Noviomagus = 'new field', ie new settlement of the Batavi (Batavians).

Nikolayev (port on *Black Sea* in republic of *Ukraine*, USSR)
Named not after one of Russian tsars Nicholas but after ship *St Nicholas* which was the first to be launched from the ship-building yard here in 1784.

Nile, River (longest river in *Africa*, rising near Lake *Victoria* and flowing north into *Mediterranean*)
One of oldest geographical names in the world; probably from Semitic-Hamitic nagal = 'river'.

Nîmes (city in south *France*, north-west of *Marseilles*)
Roman name was Nemausus, from Gaulish nem = 'sanctuary' + Latin suffix -ausum.

Nome (port in west *Alaska*, USA, on *Bering* Strait)
A 'mistake' name: written note '? name' made on chart of coastal region here by English map-maker was misread as name of cape (ie Cape Name); this was later corrupted to Cape Nome, which gave name to port.

Norfolk Island (in South *Pacific*, north-east of *Sydney*, *Australia*)
Discovered by Cook in 1774 and named by him probably not after English county of Norfolk but after 9th Duke of Norfolk.

Normandy (region and historic province in north-west *France*)
Named after Norsemen ('north men') who invaded it in 9th century and
settled here as Normans.

North Sea (between *Great Britain* and continent of *Europe*)
So named by Dutch, as Noord Zee, in contrast to *Zuider Zee* (= 'south
sea'). Roman name was Oceanus Germanicus = 'German sea'.

Norway (kingdom in north-west *Europe*)
Original name was Norreweg; Norsemen had 3 chief sea-routes to and
from *Scandinavia*: Austurweg (= 'eastern way') through the *Baltic*, Ves-
turweg (= 'western way') across *North Sea*, and Norreweg (= 'northern
way') to and from the north along the Scandinavian coast. Last of these
came to denote the coast and later, in 9th century, the territory approximating to Norway.

Nova Scotia (province in east *Canada*, on *Atlantic* coast)
Latin = 'new Scotland'. French were 1st settlers here, and called territory
Acadia. In 1621 English and Scottish king James I granted territory to
Scott Sir William Alexander, who named it, in classical style, after
his native land.

Novaya Zemlya (group of islands in *Arctic*, in north USSR)
Russian = 'new land'. English explorer Sir Hugh Willoughby, who discovered islands in 1553, reported them under this name, which was
possibly given by north coastal dwellers as long ago as 12th century.

Novgorod (city in north-west USSR, south-west of *Leningrad*)
Russian = 'new town'. Novgorod is one of most ancient of all Russian
cities (founded in 9th century). Name is common for a number of
Russian towns, eg Nizhny Novgorod (now *Gorky*), Novgorod-Seversky
in *Ukraine*, and many more. Varangians (Scandinavian Vikings who
settled in *Russia* in 9th century) called it Holmgard = 'island town'.

Nyasaland (former name of *Malawi*)
Named after Lake Nyasa, in turn with native name = 'lake'. Renamed
Malawi in 1964.

O **Ob, River** (long river in west *Siberia*, USSR, flowing north into *Arctic* Ocean)
Possibly from Iranian ab = 'water, river' or, less likely, from local (Komi) word = 'aunt'.

Oberammergau (small town and resort in *Bavaria*, West *Germany*, south-west of *Munich*)
From German ober = 'upper' + Ammer (name of river, from Old High German am = 'to flow') + Gau = 'district'.

Oceania (loose term for islands of Central and South-West *Pacific*)
Name was invented by Danish–French geographer Malte Brun (1775–1826) about 1812, and generally refers to islands of *Polynesia*, *Melanesia*, *Micronesia* and, usually, Australasia.

Odense (city and port in south-east *Denmark*)
Derived from name of Odin, great god of Scandinavian mythology (same as Woden), who was worshipped here.

Oder, River (rises in *Moravia*, *Czechoslovakia*, and flows generally north through *Poland* into *Baltic Sea*)
Probably from Indoeuropean adu = 'current', or possibly from Slavonic dr = 'wearing through, eroding'. Not likely to be from Old High German atar = 'rapid' since this would have given name as Ader.

Odessa (city and port on *Black Sea* in republic of *Ukraine*, USSR)
When town was built in 1795, by order of Catherine II, it was given, according to current fashion, name of Greek origin: in this case Odessos, as it was thought to be on site of former Greek colony of Miletus on north coast of *Black Sea* (actually west of present city). Name is often falsely linked with Greek mythical hero Odysseus. (For similar 'Greek' Russian names see *Sebastopol*, *Simferopol*.)

Ohio (river and state in north USA)
From Indian (Iroquois) word = 'beautiful' (referring to river); when French settlers explored river about 1680 they translated Indian word and

named river La Belle Rivière (= 'the beautiful river'). River gave name to state.

Oise, River (rises in *Belgium* in *Ardennes* Mountains and flows south-west into *France* to join River *Seine* just below *Pontoise*)
From Indoeuropean eiso, oiso = 'rapid'.

Okhotsk, Sea of (in North-West *Pacific*, south-east USSR, between *Sakhalin* and *Kamchatka*)
Named by Russian Cossacks after River Okata (with its own name derived from Evenki word = 'river') which flows into it. Same river is also called Okhota, a more popular name as it is (falsely) associated with Russian okhota = 'hunting'.

Oklahoma (state in south USA)
From Indian (Choctaw) okla = 'people' + homa = 'red', ie 'red-skinned people'. Name came into use as late as 1866 when it was proposed by Choctaw chief as official name for territory.

Olympia (state capital of *Washington*, USA)
Name given to city (founded 1850) after nearby Mount Olympus, so (fancifully) named by English traveller John Meares in 1788.

Olympus (mountain range in north *Greece*)
Traditional home of Greek gods in mythology; not likely to derive from Greek olympos = 'glittering' as name was known in pre-Greek times. Perhaps from Caucasian word = 'mountain'.

Omaha (largest city in *Nebraska*, USA, on River *Missouri*)
From Indian (Sioux) tribal name, perhaps = 'dwellers on the upper reaches of the river'.

Oman (sultanate in east *Arabia*)
From name of ancient city, now no longer in existence. City derived name from Arabic word, perhaps = 'stopped here' (referring to nomads who settled here), or from name of founder Oman-ben-Ibrahim.

Omdurman (city in *Sudan*, north-west of *Khartoum*)
Named after local Moslem saint Um-Marium (1646–1730)

Ontario (province in central *Canada* and lake on its south-eastern border)
From Indian (Iroquois) oniatar-io = 'beautiful' (referring to lake). Lake gave name to province. (Compare *Ohio*: ending -io is common to both.)

Oporto (city and seaport in north-west *Portugal*)
From Portuguese o porto = 'the port'. Roman name was Portus cale = 'warm harbour' (ie not freezing over), which gave name of whole country *Portugal*.

Oran (city and seaport on *Mediterranean* in north-west *Algeria*)
Either from Arabic Wahran or from Warahan, name of medieval Berber ruler. Roman name was Portus divinus = 'port of the gods'.

Orange Free State (province in South *Africa* between River *Orange* and River *Vaal*)
State is named after river, in turn named by Dutch settlers in 1777 in honour of Dutch royal house of Orange (who had owned principality of Orange in south *France* from 8th century to 1713).

Oregon (state in north-west USA, on *Pacific* coast)
Name has had derivation ascribed to numerous languages, including Spanish, French, Iranian and Indian, with meanings varying from 'hurricane' to 'piece of dried apple'. More likely (and interesting) theory is that name results from mistake of French map-engraver who in 1715 rendered River *Wisconsin* as 'Ouariconsint' with last 4 letters ('sint') on line below, thus inventing a mythical River Ouaricon, anglicised as Oregon and eventually becoming name of state.

Orinoco, River (in *Venezuela*, South *America*)
From Indian (Carib) orenoco = 'river'.

Orkney Islands (north of *Scotland*, *Great Britain*)
Of uncertain origin. Pliny wrote of them in 1st century as Orcades,

which Angles 'translated' as orku = 'dolphin' + ey = 'island', but this was merely attempt to explain unknown meaning.

Orléans (city on River *Loire*, south-west of *Paris, France*)
Gaulish name was Cenabium, from Celtic cenna = 'hill'. Original city was destroyed by Caesar and rebuilt in 3rd century as Roman fortified town with name Aurelianum, in honour of Emperor Aurelius. From this comes modern name Orléans.

Osaka (2nd largest city in *Japan*, south-west of *Tokyo*)
Name known since 14th century, when city became capital. From Japanese oo-saka = 'big hill'.

Oslo (capital of *Norway*)
Probably from Indoeuropean os = 'mouth' + name of River Lo, though could perhaps be from Norwegian ass og lo = 'forest clearing'. From 1624 to 1925 was Christiania, after King Christian IV, in whose reign it was rebuilt when earlier city had been destroyed by fire. City was first founded in 1048 by Viking Harold Hardrad.

Ostend (seaport and resort in west *Belgium*, on *North Sea*)
In Flemish Oostende = 'east end', ie either of bay or because at east end of sandbank (at west end of which is resort Westende).

Otranto, Strait of (between south-east *Italy* and *Albania*)
Strait is named after town Otranto, formerly Greek Hydruntum = 'water town' (from Greek hydor = 'water').

Ottawa (capital of *Canada*, in south-east *Ontario*)
Named after River Ottawa, in turn from Indian (Algonquian) adawe = 'big river' or possibly 'traders'. Town was founded in 1827 with name Bytown, after English colonel John By of Royal Engineers whose men built Rideau Canal here; named Ottawa in 1854 when it became capital.

P

Pacific Ocean (between *Asia* and Western *Australia* and North and South *America*)
Spanish explorer Vasco Balboa first sighted Pacific in 1513 from Panama isthmus and called it South Sea (as opposed to North Sea, ie *Atlantic*). When Magellan crossed the Ocean from *Tierra del Fuego* to *Philippines* in 1520-1 he encountered no storms and so named it Mar Pacifico = 'calm sea'.

Padua (city in north-east *Italy*, west of *Venice*)
Possibly from Latin padus = 'pine-tree' (compare *Po*), or from name of River Adda, in turn derived perhaps from padvos = 'rapid'.

Pago Pago (chief port of American *Samoa*, South *Pacific*)
From native (Polynesian) name Pango Pango. (According to story, missionaries printing news-sheet here in 19th century were short of letter 'n' so printed name without this letter.)

Pakistan (republic of South *Asia*, bordering in east with *India*)
Name was first proposed in 1931, and established with partition of *India* in 1947; possibly from Urdu or Iranian pak = 'clean' (ie in spirit) + stan = 'country', but alternative explanation says that name was devised in 1933 by group of Moslem students at Cambridge University from initial letters of Moslem states *Punjab*, *Afghanistan*, *Kashmir*, *Iran*, Sind and final element of *Baluchistan*.

Palermo (city and seaport in north-west *Sicily*, south *Italy*)
From Greek name Panormos, from pan = 'all, every' + hormos = 'harbour'. Seventeen ports with this name were known to have existed on *Mediterranean* in time of Greek empire.

Palestine (former name of *Israel*)
From ancient people, Philistines, enemies of Israelites, who inhabited south-west Palestine from the 12th century BC. Their name is from Hebrew palash = 'to travel' and so = 'wanderers'.

Palma (capital of *Majorca* and *Balearic Islands*)
Name is Roman (= 'palm') and is translation of name of Phoenician colony here, Tamar.

Pamirs (range of mountains in Central *Asia*, mainly in *Tadzhikistan*, south USSR)
Noted by Chinese travellers of 7th century as Po-mi-lo. Many explanations suggested, among which are: 1. from name Upa-Meru = 'under Meru' (mountain of Meru in Hindu mythology is centre of the world); 2. from Sanskrit mir = 'lake' (of which there are many in Pamir mountains); 3. from Po-i-mur = 'foot of death' or Po-i-murg = 'bird's foot'; 4. (more possibly) from Pa-i-mihr = 'foot of the sun', ie at the foot of Mithras, god of the sun.

Pamplona (capital of province of *Navarra*, north *Spain*)
Founded in 68 BC as Pompeiopolis = 'Pompey's town'.

Panama (republic in Central *America*)
From one of a number of like-sounding Indian words, perhaps = 'many fish' (Spanish explorers found many fishermen's huts here in 16th century). Country named after its capital, now Panama City, founded in 1519. Panama Canal is named after country.

Papua (territory on island of *New Guinea*, north of *Australia*)
From name of inhabitants, Papuans, who are native to many islands of *Melanesia* and *Polynesia*. Their name is of Malay origin, probably from papuvah = 'curly-headed', or perhaps from pua-pua = 'dark brown'.

Paraguay (republic in central South *America*)
Named after River Paraguay, in turn after native Indian tribe, Paragua, with name derived from Indian para = 'water'.

Paramaribo (capital and chief seaport of Surinam, north-east South *America*)
From Indian para = 'water, sea' + maribo = 'dwellers, inhabitants'.

Paraná (river and state in south *Brazil*, South *America*)
State—and city of Paraná, formerly Bajada de Santa Fé (= 'hill of the Holy Faith')—named after river, in turn derived from Indian para = 'water'.

Paris (capital of *France*)
Full Roman name was Lutetia Parisiorum = 'Lutetia of the Parisii'. Lutetia probably derives from Latin lutum = 'clay, sludge'. Parisii were Gaulish tribe with name perhaps deriving from Celtic par = 'ship' (ie 'shipmen, sailors', dwelling on banks of River *Seine*), or from word = 'border town'.

Parma (city in central north *Italy*)
Name is of Etruscan (pre-Roman) origin, of uncertain meaning. May be connected with Semitic (Arabic) barma = 'circle, turn', ie 'curve in the river'. Name persisted in spite of Roman renaming as Colonia Julia Augusta (= 'colony of Julius Augustus') and Greek renaming as Chryso-polis (= 'gold-town').

Parry Islands (in *Arctic*, north of *Canada*)
Named by John Ross after English polar explorer Sir William Parry (1790–1855) who discovered them in expedition of 1818–20.

Pasadena (city in *California*, USA, north-east of *Los Angeles*)
Name was artificially concocted in 1875 from 4 long Indian words ending in -pa, -sa, -de, -na, with original meaning perhaps = 'crown of the valley', 'key of the ranch' or something similar.

Patagonia (region in south of South *America* comprising *Argentina* and *Chile*)
Name was given by Portuguese explorer Magellan in 1520 during his 1st voyage round the world, from Portuguese pata = '(animal's) foot'; natives wore animal skins round their feet which left large footprints in the sand.

Paterson (city in north-east *New Jersey*, USA)
Named in 1791 in honour of Governor William Paterson (1745–1806).

Peking (capital of *China*)
From Chinese bei = 'north' + kin (tsing) = 'capital'; ie 'northern capital' (as distinct from *Nanking*). Alternative name of Peiping has same meaning.

Peloponnese (south peninsula of *Greece*)
From Greek = 'island of Pelops': Greek nesos = 'island' + Pelops, in Greek mythology the son of Tantalus, who in a chariot race beat King Oenomaus and won the hand of his daughter and this territory. Name is good example of a myth evolving from a place-name whose true meaning is unknown.

Pemba (island in Indian Ocean, north-east of *Zanzibar*, off east coast of *Tanzania*)
Name is from a Bantu language, as yet unexplained. Arabic names for island are Jezirat-el-khazra = 'emerald island' and Jezirat-el-khutra = 'green island'.

Pennsylvania (state in north-east USA, bordering on Lake *Erie*)
Territory to west of River *Delaware* was granted in 1681 by English king Charles II to Quaker William Penn after whom, + element derived from Latin silva = 'wood', it was named, ie 'Penn's woodland'. (Penn himself claimed that 1st element derived not from his own name but from Celtic pen = 'headland'.)

Périgueux (town in central south-west *France*, south-west of *Limoges*)
Name is derived from that of Gaulish tribe Petrocorii, whose own name was mentioned by Livy as Tricori (= 'three armies'), from Gaulish corio = 'army' which became final element (-gueux) of modern name.

Pernambuco (state in north-east *Brazil*, South *America*)
Named after former capital, now *Recife*, from Indian parana = 'big river' (compare *Paraná*) + mbucu = 'arm'; town was built on delta of two rivers. Less likely derivation is from Indian peranabuco = 'stone with a hole bored through it'.

Persia (former name, still sometimes used, of *Iran*)
From name of one of peoples, Farsi (after whom also is named province Fars in south of country), whose own name is of uncertain origin, though has been linked with Pharisees and with Sanskrit parasah = 'steed' (ie 'horsemen'). Name was regarded as unsuitable and officially changed to *Iran* in 1935.

Perth (capital of Western *Australia*, near coast of Indian Ocean)
Founded in 1829 by Scottish settlers and named by governor of colony Scottish captain James Stirling after his native town of Perth.

Peru (republic in west of South *America*)
Name was given in 16th century by Spanish settlers, after River Biru, where they landed after sailing here from *Panama* isthmus. Name of river probably derives either from Indian word = 'river' or from name of Indian chief. Incas, encountered here by Spanish explorers, called their country Tahuantin-suyn = 'four provinces'.

Peshawar (city in north-west *Pakistan*, north-west of *Lahore*)
From Sanskrit purasha-pura = 'frontier town'.

Petrograd (former name of *Leningrad*, USSR)
Name *St Petersburg* came to be regarded in 1914 as too 'Germanic', so was changed to Slavonic variant Petrograd, with same basic meaning ('Peter's town'). Renamed *Leningrad* in 1924.

Philadelphia (largest city in *Pennsylvania*, USA)
Founded by English Quaker William Penn in 1682 with name, expressing his religious ideals, derived from Greek = 'brotherly love'. No doubt Penn also had biblical city of Philadelphia in mind.

Philippines (group of islands in South-West *Pacific*, and republic which they form)
Discovered by Magellan in 1521 who named them St Lazarus Islands after saint's day, 17 December, on which he sighted them. Twenty-two years later, when settled by Spanish, they were renamed after heir to Spanish throne, future king Philip II.

Phnom-Penh (capital of *Cambodia*)
Khmer words = 'mountain of abundance'.

Phoenix (state capital of *Arizona*, USA)
Name not connected with Greek Phoenicia (although inhabitants are known as Phoenicians). Connection with phoenix, mythological bird, seems inappropriate, as city has never risen from the ashes (ie been rebuilt after a fire). But perhaps it was built on site of a burned-down Indian village.

Picardy (historic province in north-east *France*)
From Old French pic = 'pike, lance', name given to inhabitants who in 13th century were armed with pikes.

Piedmont (region in north *Italy*, bordering on *Switzerland* and *France*)
From Old Italian pie di monte = 'foot of the mountain' (ie *Alps*).

Pierre (state capital of South *Dakota*, USA)
Named after Pierre Choteau of American Fur Company which built fort here in 1832.

Pietermaritzburg (capital of province of *Natal*, South *Africa*, west of *Durban*)
Founded in 1838 by 'voortrekker' Boers Pieter Retief and Gert Maritz. Name is often shortened to Maritzburg.

Pisa (city in *Tuscany*, north *Italy*, south-west of *Florence*)
One of 12 Etruscan towns of this name, as yet not satisfactorily explained (perhaps = 'river mouth').

Pitcairn Island (in South *Pacific*, midway between *Australia* and South *America*)
Discovered by English explorer Philip Carteret in 1767 who named it after midshipman who first sighted it.

Pittsburgh (city in south-west *Pennsylvania*, USA)
Founded by French settlers in 1754 with name Fort Duquesne, after

governor of French *Canada*. Captured by English in 1758 and renamed Pittsburgh in honour of English statesman William Pitt (1708–78) as compliment for his support against French forces.

Plate, River (estuary of River *Paraná* and River *Uruguay*, South *America*, flowing south-east between *Uruguay* and *Argentina* into *Atlantic*) Spanish name, Rio de la Plata = 'river of silver', was given by Sebastian Cabot in 1526 when he discovered it and here bartered with natives for silver. (See *Argentina*.)

Plenty, Bay of (on north-east coast of North Island, *New Zealand*) So named by Cook in 1770 on account of numerous flourishing villages observed by him along coast here, with whose inhabitants he had had profitable dealings.

Plovdiv (2nd largest city in *Bulgaria*, south-east of *Sofia*) Founded (or rebuilt) in 359 BC by Macedonian king Philip II, after whom it was originally named, as Philippopolis (= 'Philip's town'), or, in local language of Daco-Moesian, Pulpudava, with same meaning (Pulp = 'Philip' + dava = 'town'). Latter name persisted and became modern Plovdiv, although Romans renamed town as Trimontium (= 'with three hills').

Po, River (in north *Italy* flowing east into *Adriatic Sea*) From Latin name Padus, of uncertain origin; perhaps from Ligurian bodincus, bodeghos = 'bottomless' or from Gaulish padi = 'pine', which is probably origin of city of *Padua*.

Poitiers (town in central west *France*, south-east of *Nantes*) Before Roman occupation was (in Latin version) Lemonum, probably from Gaulish leima = 'lime-tree'. It was territory of Gaulish tribe Pictavi (Pictones), from whose name modern Poitiers evolved.

Poitou (historic province in west *France*, part of *Aquitaine*) From Latin Pictavum, of same origin as that of its capital, *Poitiers*.

Poland (republic in east central *Europe*)
From inhabitants, Poles, with name derived from Slavonic polyane =
'plain dwellers'. Country is largely low-lying.

Polynesia (large group of islands in Central and South-East *Pacific*, in-
cluding *Hawaii*, *Samoa* and *Tonga*)
From Greek polys = 'many' + nesos = 'island'; name was first used by
Portuguese explorer Barros in 16th century but applied only to large
islands between *Asia* and *Australia*. Name served as 'model'—as did
Oceania—for *Micronesia*, *Melanesia* and *Indonesia*.

Pomerania (region in north central *Europe* bordering on *Baltic Sea*,
mainly in *Poland*)
From Slavonic pomorye = 'region by the sea'. Polish name of region is
Pomorze.

Pondicherry (territory and its capital in south-east *India*)
Originally Poducheri = 'new town', from Tamil podupudu = 'new' +
cheri = 'town'.

Pontoise (town in north *France* on River *Oise*, north of *Paris*)
From Latin pontus (French pont) = 'bridge' + name of River *Oise*.

Popocatapetl (volcano in *Mexico*, south-east of Mexico City)
From Aztec popocani = 'to smoke' + tepetl = 'mountain', ie 'smoking
mountain'.

Port Arthur (former name of Chinese port *Lushun*)
Named after English captain Arthur who surveyed coast here in 1860.
Together with *Talien* (formerly *Dairen* or *Dalny*) now forms part of large
port of *Lü-ta*.

Port-au-Prince (capital of *Haiti*, *West Indies*)
French = 'port of the Prince'; story is that ship named *Prince*, probably
French but possibly English, had taken shelter in bay on which town is
now situated. Bay was called Le Port du Prince and in 1743 French
authorities decided to make town that had arisen here the capital of

Saint-Domingue (present *Haiti*). Name, which had already become Port-au-Prince, was formalised by French royal decree in 1749.

Port Elizabeth (seaport in *Cape Province*, South *Africa*, east of *Capetown*)
Founded by English settlers in 1820 and planned by Sir Rufane Donkin who named it after his late wife.

Port Harcourt (seaport in south-east *Nigeria*, West *Africa*)
Founded in 1914 and named after then British Colonial Secretary Sir William Harcourt.

Port Moresby (chief seaport of *New Guinea*, in south-east of the island)
Named after British explorer John Moresby (1830–1922) who discovered harbour here, on which town now stands, in 1873.

Porto Novo (capital and seaport of *Dahomey*, West *Africa*)
Portuguese = 'new harbour'; so named by Portuguese slave-traders who landed here in 15th century.

Port Phillip (inlet of *Bass Strait*, south *Victoria*, *Australia*)
Originally named Port King by Lieutenant Murray, who discovered it in 1801, after the then governor, but later changed name to Port Phillip in honour of Captain Arthur Phillip (1738–1814), British founder and 1st governor of *New South Wales*.

Port Said (city and seaport on *Mediterranean* at entrance to *Suez* Canal, *Egypt*)
Founded in 1860 when *Suez* Canal was begun by French diplomat Ferdinand de Lesseps and named by him after Pasha Said, then Viceroy (Khedive) of *Egypt*.

Portugal (republic in south-west *Europe*)
Name derives from port of Portus Cale (modern *Oporto*), with its own name from Latin = 'warm harbour' (ie ice-free). Town was captured by Moors in 11th century and gave its name first to surrounding territory, then to whole country.

Potomac, River (in east USA, flowing into *Chesapeake Bay*)
Name is of Indian origin, but of uncertain meaning. Perhaps a tribal
name. Recorded by English explorer John Smith in 1608 as Patawomeck.

Potsdam (city in north of West *Germany*, south-west of *Berlin*)
In 993 was Poztupimi. Possibly from Slavonic pod dubimi = 'under the
oak-trees', but more likely from personal name Postamp.

Poznan (city in west *Poland*)
Probably from personal name Poznan, 1st settler here.

Prague (capital of *Czechoslovakia*)
Many theories as to origin; perhaps connected with Czech praziti =
'place where wood has been burned', or with Slavonic prati = 'to work'
(referring to fish-dykes constructed in river).

Pretoria (capital of South *Africa*, and of *Transvaal*)
Founded and named, in 1855, in honour of Andries Pretorius (1799–
1853), Boer leader, by his son, the 1st president of *Transvaal*.

Prince Albert (town in central *Saskatchewan, Canada*)
Founded in 1866 as mission station and named after English prince consort
Albert, husband of Queen Victoria (compare Lake *Albert, Africa*).

Prince Edward Island (province of east *Canada*, in Gulf of *St Lawrence*)
Discovered by French explorer Jacques Cartier in 1534, who named it
Île St Jean, anglicised as St John's Island when ceded to *Britain* in 1763.
In 1798 renamed Prince Edward Island in honour of English prince
Edward (1767–1820), 4th son of King George III and father of Queen
Victoria.

Prince of Wales Island (north of Cape *York, Queensland, Australia*)
Discovered by Cook in 1770 and named by him in honour of Prince of
Wales, future English king George IV.

Provence (historic province in south-east *France*)
From Latin provincia = 'province'. South Gaul, as part of Roman empire,

was called Provincia Narboniensis (after town of Narbonne) and was originally much larger territory than modern Provence, extending from *Alps* to *Pyrenees*.

Providence (state capital of *Rhode Island*, USA)
So named by English settler Roger Williams in 1636, to express 'God's merciful providence' in delivering him from hostile Indian tribesmen.

Prussia (former principal state of *Germany*)
Named after inhabitants, Prussians, who dwelt on south-east coast of *Baltic Sea*. Their name derives from Lithuanian prud, prut = 'pond, lake'.

Puebla (state and its capital in central *Mexico*, Central *America*)
From Spanish pueblo = 'village, settlement'. Town was founded in 1531 by Franciscan friar T. Motolineo with name Puebla de los Angeles = 'town of the angels', from belief that angels helped in construction of church here. City gave name to state.

Puerto Rico (island in *West Indies*)
Spanish = 'rich port'; originally name of bay on north coast discovered and named by Columbus in 1493 (though island itself he named San Juan = 'Saint John', as he landed here on St John's Day, 24 June). Name of bay became that of town founded in 1508 by Ponce de Leon, its 1st governor, then spread to whole island. From 1898 to 1932 was known as Porto Rico.

Punjab (state, former province, in north-west *India*)
From Iranian penj = 'five' + ab = 'water', ie 'five rivers' (Jhelum, Chenab, Ravi, Beas and Sutlej, all tributaries of River *Indus*).

Pusan (city and chief seaport of South *Korea*, on south-east coast)
From Japanese = 'pot-mountain', probably with reference to pot-shaped mountain at foot of which city is situated.

Pushkin (town in north-west USSR, south of *Leningrad*)
Named (since 1937) after Russian national poet Alexander Pushkin, who

spent childhood years here. From 1918 to 1937 was Detskoye Selo = 'children's village': town was planned to be holiday centre for children. Before 1918 was Tsarskoye Selo; from 18th century was country residence of Russian royal family, although name was not derived from word tsar but from Estonian saari = 'island, hill', and in 1708 was recorded as Sarskoye Selo.

Pyongyang (capital of North *Korea*, north-west of *Seoul*)
From Korean p'hyon = 'plain'.

Pyrenees (range of mountains in South-west *Europe* dividing *France* from *Spain*)
Probably from Basque pyren or Celtic byrin = 'mountain'.

Quebec (province and its capital in east *Canada*)
Probably from Indian quilibek = 'place where the river narrows' (ie River *St Lawrence*), but perhaps from word = 'place of shooting'. City was founded in 1608 by French coloniser Samuel de Champlain.

Queen Charlotte Islands (off coast of British *Columbia*, *Canada*)
Named by English captain Dixon in 1787 after his ship, the *Queen Charlotte*, in turn named after Queen Charlotte, wife of King George III.

Queen Maud Land (Norwegian territory in *Antarctic*)
Discovered by Norwegian expedition of Rieser and Larsen in 1930 and named after Queen Maud, wife of Norwegian king Haakon VII.

Queensland (state in north-east *Australia*)
Formed part of colony of *New South Wales* until 1859 when became separate colony named in honour of Queen Victoria. (Originally, name of Cooksland had been proposed, but was rejected in favour of Queensland.)

Quetta (city in central west *Pakistan*)
From Iranian word, in Arabic variant, = 'fortress'.

Quimper (town in *Brittany*, north-west *France*, south-east of *Brest*)
From Breton cenbera = 'confluence'; town is at point where River Odet
joins River Steir.

Quito (capital of *Ecuador*, South *America*)
Was name of whole country until 1830; city was named Quito by
Spanish explorers in 1533 after Indian Quitu tribe who inhabited territory
(but who were extinct by end of Spanish rule in 1822).

R

Rabat (capital of *Morocco*, North-West *Africa*)
Founded in 1306. Possibly from Arabic = 'place of faith' or, more likely,
'small town'. Similar name was given by Arabs to settlements established
in conquered lands.

Raleigh (state capital of North *Carolina*, USA)
Named in 1792 in honour of Sir Walter Raleigh who more than 200
years earlier had made several unsuccessful attempts to colonise '*Virginia*'
(present North *Carolina*).

Rangoon (capital of *Burma*)
Probably named after pagoda of Dagon (god with name from Burmese
takun = 'tree-trunk'), or possibly from Burmese yangun = 'peaceful',
though this could be attempt to explain unknown name.

Ravenna (city in north-east *Italy*, south-east of *Bologna*)
Name existed BC and is probably of Etruscan origin, but of unknown
meaning. Ending -enna is common to many names of Asia Minor and
suggests language group common to *Mediterranean* countries.

Recife (capital of *Pernambuco*, north-east *Brazil*, South *America*)
First settled by Portuguese about 1535 who named it Ciudad de Recife =
'reef town'. Earlier (Indian) name was *Pernambuco*.

Red Sea (between North-East *Africa* and South-East *Asia*)
Several possible explanations: 1. because of reddish colour of water
caused by brightly-coloured shells; 2. from reddish colour of banks;

3. from name of ancient tribe of Himarites (= 'red'); 4. with meaning 'southern', as many Asian and African peoples denoted countries by colours, with red = south, black = north, etc (compare *Black Sea*).

Reggio di Calabria (city in *Calabria*, south *Italy*, on Strait of *Messina*)
From Latin regium = 'royal town, royal castle' + name of region *Calabria*. Town was founded about 700 BC as Greek colony.

Regina (capital of province of *Saskatchewan, Canada*)
Latin = 'queen'. Name was suggested in 1882 by Princess Louise, wife of Governor General Lord Lorne (see also *Alberta*) as compliment to Queen Victoria (whose own name was already widespread as a place-name).

Réunion (island in Indian Ocean, south-west of *Mauritius*)
French = 'reunion'. Discovered by Magellan in early 16th century and originally named after him. Annexed by French in 1639, who in 1649 named it Bourbon, after French royal house. In 1793, year of French Revolution, was renamed Réunion to mark union of revolutionaries from *Marseilles* with National Guard in *Paris* on 10 August previous year. (With restoration of monarchy, name reverted to Bourbon, but with revolution of 1848 was re-established as Réunion.)

Reykjavik (capital of *Iceland*)
From Icelandic reyka = 'to smoke' (referring to steam of geysers) + Old Norse vik = 'inlet'.

Rheims (city in north-east *France*, north-east of *Paris*)
Named after Gaulish tribe Remi, mentioned by Caesar in 51 BC, whose capital it was. (Tribal name may = 'rulers'.) Earlier Roman name of 1st century BC was Durocortorum, from Gaulish durum = 'fortress'.

Rhine, River (in central and west *Europe*, flowing north-west from *Alps* into *North Sea*)
From Old High German ri = 'to go, to flow' + Gaulish element (r)enos = 'water'.

Rhode Island (state in *New England*, north-east USA, bordering on *Atlantic*)
Discovered in 1524 by Italian explorer Giovanni da Verrazano who noted that island was 'about the size of the island of Rhodes' (ie Greek island in *Mediterranean*). But in 1635 Dutch settlers were calling island rode = 'red', probably referring to colour of earth. So name seems to have two origins, with 1st probably influencing 2nd.

Rhodes (largest island in *Dodecanese*, off south-west coast of *Turkey*)
Probably from Greek rhodon = 'rose', as this flower once grew in abundance here, though this could be attempt to explain earlier pre-Greek name of unknown meaning.

Rhodesia (state in south-east Central *Africa*)
Named in 1884 after Cecil Rhodes (1853–1902), British founder of South Africa Company, who administered it.

Rhône, River (river in west *Europe* rising in *Switzerland* and flowing through Lake *Geneva* into *France* and then south into *Mediterranean*)
Latin name was Rhodanus, possibly from Indoeuropean erer = 'to flow' or perhaps from Celtic rho = 'to flow quickly' (in contrast to slower flowing *Saône*, its chief tributary). Name could also be of pre-Indoeuropean (Ligurian) origin.

Rialto (commercial region in *Venice*, *Italy*, consisting of an island with surrounding district)
From Italian ripa alta = 'high bank'. Rialto Bridge over Grand Canal is named after island.

Richmond (state capital of *Virginia*, USA)
So named in 1737 by English settler William Byrd, probably because of similarity between situation of American town on River James to that of English town Richmond in Surrey on River *Thames*.

Riga (capital of republic of *Latvia*, north-west USSR)
Founded at end of 12th century on River Dvina. Name probably derives

from Slavonic reka = 'river', referring not to River Dvina, but to another river, the Reka, which has silted up and no longer exists.

Rio de Janeiro (chief seaport and former capital of *Brazil*, South *America*, on South *Atlantic*)
Portuguese members of expedition of Italian navigator Amerigo Ves-pucci sighted bay on which town is now situated on 1 January 1502 and took it for the estuary of a large river. They therefore named it Rio de Janeiro = 'January river'. Town was founded in 1566 and took this name.

Rio de Oro (coastal territory in south Spanish *Sahara*, West *Africa*)
Portuguese expedition of 1436 discovered here a long stretch of water in the desert which they took for a river, therefore naming it Rio de Oro = 'river of gold' (referring to golden sand).

Rio Grande (river rising in *Colorado*, USA, and flowing south-east through *Mexico* into Gulf of *Mexico*)
Spanish = 'great river'. Many South American rivers have this name. Mexican name is Rio Bravo = 'stormy river'.

Rio Tinto (river in south-west *Spain* and town on it)
Spanish = 'coloured river'; river is yellowish from copper mined here.

Riviera, the (name of south coastal strip with popular resorts in many countries, but notably in *France*, where it extends along *Mediterranean* coast from *Marseilles* to La Spezia, *Italy*)
Italian = 'coast'.

Rochester (city in *New York* state, USA, on Lake *Ontario*)
Originally Rochesterville when named in 1817 after Colonel Nathaniel Rochester, one of owners of territory here. Name became Rochester in 1822. (Most other American towns Rochester are named after this one, but not Rochester, *Massachusetts*, which was named in 1686 by settlers from English town Rochester, Kent.)

Romania (more correct spelling of *Rumania*)

Rome (capital of *Italy*)
Named after River Ruma, ancient name of River *Tiber*, with name probably of Etruscan origin, or possibly from Greek rheo = 'to flow'. According to tradition, Rome was founded by Romulus, son of Greek god Mars, and was named after him, but he was mythical figure.

Ross Dependency (sector of *Antarctic*, south of *New Zealand*, to whom it belongs)
Ross Sea was discovered in 1841 by English polar explorer James Ross (1800–62) after whom it, Ross Island and Ross Dependency are named.

Rotterdam (chief seaport of *Netherlands*)
Named after River Rotte, which joins River Maas (*Meuse*) at point where city stands, + dam (compare *Amsterdam*). Name of river is probably derived from Indoeuropean roth = 'hurrying'.

Rouen (city in north *France*, north-west of *Paris*)
Roman name was Rotomagus, probably from name of Gaulish tribe or person, or perhaps from Gaulish rot = 'town' + magos = 'field'.

Ruhr (river in north-west of West *Germany*, and industrial region mainly in its valley)
River gave name to region, with name derived from Indoeuropean reu = 'to dig up, excavate'.

Rumania (republic in south-east *Europe*)
Was an outpost of Roman empire early AD; native population, Dacians (Roman province was called Dacia), mingled with Roman settlers, began to speak a form of Latin, and called themselves Romani, ie 'people from Rome'. From their name comes modern name Rumania (more correctly Romania).

Russia (alternative name in many contexts for USSR, and country's official name before 1917)
Name has been in use since 15th century for whole country, from earlier name Rus, after inhabitants of same name. Origin of name is still un-

certain; possible explanations are: 1. name given by Slavs to Varangians (Swedish Vikings) whose leaders were first princes of Kievan Russia in 9th century, with meaning = 'foreigners'; 2. from Swedish tribe Ruotsi (= 'rowers'), oarsmen of Viking ships. The 1st of these theories seems more likely as Varangians came from coastal district of Roslagen (present south-east *Sweden*), and may have derived their name from 1st element of this.

Ruwenzori Range (mountain massif on *Zaire–Uganda* frontier, Central *Africa*)
Perhaps from African words = 'lord of the clouds', from element ru (see *Rwanda*).

Rwanda (republic in Central *Africa*)
From name of inhabitants, of uncertain meaning. Element ru appears in many names of Rwanda, *Uganda*, *Tanzania*, *Rhodesia* and *Zaire* (eg *Ruwenzori* Mountains, River Ruiru, River Rufiji, Mount Rungwe).

S **Saar, River** (in west *Europe* rising in *Vosges* and flowing through *France* into West *Germany* to become tributary of River *Moselle*)
Probably from Indoeuropean ser = 'to flow'. River has given its name to Saarland, coalmining region in west of West *Germany*.

Sacramento (state capital of *California*, USA)
Spanish = 'sacrament'. Name was originally given to River Sacramento in 1808 with some kind of religious association (probably with Holy Sacrament). River gave name to city.

Sahara (largest desert in world, in North *Africa*)
From Arabic sahr = 'desert' (with basic meaning 'brownish'). Name said to have been given to this particular desert by Ibn-al-Hakam in 9th century.

Saigon (capital of South *Vietnam*)
Named after River Saigon, on whose estuary it is situated. Name of

river probably = 'sandy shore' or 'shore dam', but 2nd element also = 'river', in which case meaning is perhaps 'west river'.

St Bernard Pass (1. Great St Bernard: through *Alps* on Swiss–Italian frontier; 2. Little St Bernard: through *Alps* on French–Italian frontier south of *Mont Blanc*)
Both passes named after hospices founded about 960 by St Bernard of Menthon (923–1008).

St Cloud (suburb of west *Paris, France*)
Named after St Clodvald who built a monastery here in 6th century.

St Denis (large suburb of north *Paris, France*, on River *Seine*)
Named after St Denis (Greek Dionysius), 1st bishop of Paris and patron saint of *France*, who was martyred at place now called Montmartre (= 'martyr's mount') by the Romans about 258.

St Etienne (city in central south *France*, south-west of *Lyons*)
French = 'St Stephen', to whom town was dedicated when founded in 11th century.

St Gotthard Pass (through *Alps* in south-east *Switzerland*)
Named after nearby chapel and hospice built in 11th century and dedicated to Bishop of Hildesheim, St Gotthard (Godehard) (died 1038).

St Helena (island in South *Atlantic*, west of *Angola*)
Discovered by Portuguese navigator João da Nova on St Helena's Day (22 May) 1502.

St John, River (on frontier of *Canada* and USA flowing south east through *New Brunswick* into *Atlantic*)
Discovered by French explorer Champlain on St John's Day (24 June) 1604. Named after river is city of St John, *New Brunswick*, founded in 1783 as Parr Town, after governor, Colonel Parr, but in 1785 renamed St John.

St Kitts (one of *Leeward Islands*, *West Indies*)
Discovered by Columbus in 1493 and named after his patron saint (and himself: Kit is familiar English name for Christopher).

St Lawrence (river and seaway in north-east *Canada*)
Seaway was explored by French navigator Jacques Cartier in 1534 and named after St Lawrence, on whose feast-day (10 August) he first sighted it. He named river after seaway the following year.

St Louis (largest city in *Missouri*, USA)
Founded by French fur trading company in 1764 and named in honour of French king Louis IX ('Saint Louis') and as patriotic tribute to reigning king Louis XV (1710–74).

St Lucia (one of *Windward Islands*, *West Indies*, south of *Martinique*)
Discovered by Columbus in 1502 and named after St Lucy (Spanish Santa Lucia), Sicilian virgin martyr, on whose feast-day (13 December), he landed here.

St Malo (seaport on English Channel in north *Brittany*, *France*)
Named after Maclovius, bishop of nearby Aleth (present St Servan) in 6th century.

St Moritz (resort in *Switzerland*)
Named after river, in turn named after abbey, founded in 515 but no longer in existence, dedicated to St Maurice (German St Moritz).

St Nazaire (seaport at mouth of River *Loire*, west *France*)
Named after St Nazarius, early Italian martyr, to whom church built here in 11th century was dedicated.

St Paul (state capital of *Minnesota*, USA)
Named after mission church built here in 1841 by French priest Lucien Galtier and dedicated to St Paul.

St Petersburg (1) (former name of *Leningrad*, USSR)
Founded by Tsar Peter the Great in 1703 with German-style name

(Russian Sankt-Peterburg) = 'St Peter's town', after church of St Peter and St Paul in fortress here built to defend mouth of River Neva (and doubtless also to act as fitting reminder of its founder). Was capital of *Russia* from 1713 to 1918, having been renamed *Petrograd* in 1914. (See also *Leningrad*.)

St Petersburg (2) (town in west *Florida*, USA, on Gulf of *Mexico*)
So named in 1875 by Peter Demons, president of local rail company, after his former home town of St Petersburg in *Russia*.

St Pierre and Miquelon (group of islands off south *Newfoundland*, North *Atlantic*)
Portuguese explorer Joãs Alvarez Faguendez landed on St Pierre on 21 October 1520 and named islands Eleven Thousand Virgins after feast-day, that of St Ursula and the (11,000) virgin martyrs, on which landing was made. Reason for change to St Pierre not clear; perhaps one of Portuguese navigators was named San Pedro. Name was recorded by French explorer Jacques Cartier who landed here in 1536 as 'ysles Sainct Pierre'. Name of Miquelon is similarly obscure: perhaps is diminutive of Miguel (or Miquel), name of earlier Portuguese navigator.

St Quentin (town in north-east *France* on River *Somme*)
Named after St Quintin, martyred here in 3rd century by Roman emperor Diocletian.

St Tropez (resort in south *France* on *Mediterranean*, south-west of *Cannes*)
Named after Roman martyr Torpes of Pisa (died 1st century). Church dedicated to him was built here in 1055.

St Vincent (one of *Windward Islands*, *West Indies*)
Name probably given by Columbus who landed here on St Vincent's Day (22 January) 1498.

Sakhalin (island off east coast of *Siberia*, USSR, in Sea of *Okhotsk*)
Probably from Sahalyanula = 'black river', Manchurian name of River Amur, opposite whose estuary island lies.

Salem (state capital of *Oregon*, USA)
Named after Salem, *Massachusetts*, in 1840s, which in turn was named by English Puritan settlers in 1629 knowing that this Hebrew word = 'peace' and that it was short variant of *Jerusalem*.

Salisbury (capital of *Rhodesia*, Central *Africa*)
Not named, as are 4 towns Salisbury in USA, after English city, but after Lord Salisbury, English prime minister when city was founded in 1890 (with original name of Fort Salisbury).

Salonika (city and seaport in north-east *Greece*, capital of *Macedonia*)
May derive from name of beautiful Thessalonica, sister of Alexander the Great, who was married by Cassander, the son of one of his generals and later king of *Macedonia*. Or from victory (Greek nike = 'victory') over the Thessalonians. The 1st version is more likely as King Cassander founded the city in 315 BC. Greek name of city is Thessaloniki.

Salt Lake City (state capital of *Utah*, USA)
Founded by Brigham Young in 1847 as Mormon capital with name New Jerusalem. Present name derives from nearby Great Salt Lake.

Salvador (republic in Central *America*, on *Pacific*)
Spanish = 'saviour' (ie Christ); name was given by Spanish settlers to their fort here in 1524 and gradually spread to whole territory.

Salzburg (city in *Austria*, south-west of *Vienna*)
From German Salz = 'salt' + Burg = 'town'. City has long been famed for its mining and trading of salt.

Samoa (group of islands in South *Pacific*, north-east of *Fiji*)
Name possibly given by Maoris who came from *New Zealand* to settle here and were impressed by large numbers of moas (gigantic birds of ostrich family, now extinct). More likely, moa became the totemic bird of the natives who named islands Samoa = 'place of Moa'.

San Antonio (city in *Texas*, USA, west of *Houston*)
Named after river discovered by Spanish explorers on St Anthony's Day (19 May) 1691.

Sandwich Islands (former name of *Hawaii*)
So named by Cook in 1778 in honour of First Lord of British Admiralty Earl of Sandwich (1718–92). Name fell out of use after Cook was killed here in 1779 and earlier native name of *Hawaii* was readopted.

San Francisco (seaport in *California*, USA, north-west of *Los Angeles*)
Name (Spanish = 'St Francis') is connected with Francis in two ways: 1. Spanish Franciscan monks set up missionary station here in 1776, but also 2. Sir Francis Drake had landed here earlier, in 1578, when bay was named Port Sir Francis. Name San Francisco was officially adopted by city in 1847.

San José (capital of *Costa Rica*, Central *America*)
Spanish = 'St Joseph'. City was founded by Spanish in 1736, originally with name Villa Nueva = 'new town'; name was later changed to San José.

San Juan (capital of *Puerto Rico*, *West Indies*)
Named after founder of city in 1521, Spanish explorer Juan Ponce de León, who is buried here.

San Marino (republic within *Italy*, south-west of Rimini, near *Adriatic* coast)
Said to have been founded about AD 300 as a religious community on Monte Titano by St Marinus (Italian San Marino), a stone-cutter.

San Remo (port and resort in north-west *Italy*, south-west of Genoa)
Originally known as San Romulo (Italian = 'St Romulus'), bishop who founded it in 6th century. In 15th century became San Remo (= 'St Remus'), possibly by confusion with French St Remi (Remigius), or perhaps through contraction of Latin Sancti Romuli in Eremo = '(church) of the hermitage of St Romulus'.

San Salvador (capital of *Salvador*, Central *America*)
Spanish = 'holy saviour' (ie Christ). Name was given by Spanish settlers who founded city in 1526 on Feast of Transfiguration (6 August).

Santa Cruz (city in central *Bolivia*, South *America*)
Spanish = 'holy cross'. City was founded by Spanish missionaries on Holy Cross Day (14 September) 1560.

Santa Fé (state capital of *New Mexico*, USA)
Spanish = 'holy faith'. Founded by Spanish missionaries in 1609 and given, like *Sacramento* and other towns named Santa Fé in USA and *Argentina*, a name of religious significance.

Santiago (capital of *Chile*, South *America*)
City was founded in 1541 by Spanish conqueror Pedro de Valdivia and named in honour of St James (Spanish San Jago), saint of special significance to the Spanish people as, according to tradition, it is said that he visited *Spain* and preached the gospel there, and that after his martyrdom his body was brought to *Spain* from *Jerusalem*. It is still venerated in the shrine of Santiago de Compostela, *Galicia*, once one of the chief places, with *Jerusalem* and *Rome*, of European Christian pilgrimage.

Santo Domingo (capital of *Dominican Republic*, *West Indies*)
Spanish = 'holy Sunday'. City was founded on a Sunday in 1496 by Spanish missionaries. From 1936 to 1961 was known as Ciudad Trujillo, after president and dictator Trujillo Molina (assassinated 1961).

Saône, River (in *France* rising in the *Vosges* and joining River *Rhône* at *Lyons*)
Oldest known name of river is Brigoulos; Roman name was Arar, from Indoeuropean ar = 'to flow'. From 4th century became Sauconne, from Gaulish soghan = 'calm' (in contrast to *Rhône*).

São Paulo (state and its capital in south-east *Brazil*, South *America*)
Portuguese = 'St Paul'. City was founded by Jesuit monks in 1554 who celebrated first mass here on St Paul's Day (25 January).

Saragossa (city in north-east *Spain*, on River *Ebro*, west of *Barcelona*)
Before Roman occupation was Salduba. In 27 BC was renamed, as were many towns throughout Roman empire about this time, in honour of Emperor Augustus, with full name Caesarea Augusta. This name, over the centuries, and corrupted by Goths, Arabs and Spanish, resulted in modern name of Saragossa. Spanish name of city is Zaragoza.

Sardinia (2nd largest island in *Mediterranean*, south of *Corsica*)
Name probably derives from Sardi, Iberian tribe who inhabited north *Egypt* in 14th century BC. Link is also possible with Carthaginian sarado = 'foot' (referring to outline of island), and other ancient names of island are close to this in meaning, eg Ichnusa = 'footprint', Sandaliotis = 'sandal-shaped'.

Sargasso Sea (region of North *Atlantic* extending east off coast of *Florida*, USA)
Named after its floating seaweed (*Sargassum bacciferum*), with its own name derived from Portuguese sargaço, from resemblance of bubbles of air on the seaweed to the 'sarga' grape. Sea was named after Columbus's expedition of 1492.

Saskatchewan (central southern province of *Canada*)
Named after River Saskatchewan, in turn with name derived from Indian word; possibly from susquehanna = 'winding river', kisiskachewan = 'fast-flowing river' or siskachiwan = 'great rapids'.

Saskatoon (2nd largest city in *Saskatchewan*, *Canada*)
From Indian (Cree) misaskwatomin = 'fruit of the tree of much wood'. Name of city is used for the serviceberry (kind of shadbush) and its fruit, which grows abundantly in region.

Saudi Arabia (kingdom in South-West *Asia*)
From name of King Ibn-Saud, who in 1932 founded kingdom from two former states of Nejd and Hejas.

Savoy (former duchy, now two departments, in south-east *France*)
From Swiss dialect word zaù, dsaù = 'uplands, mountains' (ie *Alps*).

Saxony (former 'Land' of *Germany*, in south of East *Germany*)
Named after Saxons, Germanic people who once inhabited it, having
come south from north-west *Germany* in 3rd century BC; their name
derives from Old High German sahs = 'stone sword' (weapon with
which they fought).

Scandinavia (peninsula of north-west *Europe* comprising *Norway* and
Sweden)
Pliny wrote of 'an island of unknown size named Scatinavia'. Ending is
Latin suffix -ia denoting territory; middle element -av- is from Old
Norse ey = 'island'; 1st element scan(din) is unexplained (meaning 'good'
has been suggested).

Scapa Flow (stretch of sea in *Orkney Islands*, north of *Scotland*, *Great
Britain*)
From English scape = 'channel' + Flow in sense of 'current'. Not likely
to be from Germanic skapa = 'cliff, rock'.

Scheldt, River (rising in north-east *France* and flowing north-east
through *Belgium* into south *Netherlands* and *North Sea*)
All versions of name—English Scheldt; Dutch, Flemish, German Schelde;
French Escaut—probably derive from medieval Latin form of name
Scaldis = 'shallow'.

Schleswig-Holstein ('Land' in north of West *Germany*, south of *Denmark*)
Name is formed from two historic territories, independent up to 1386
as duchies of Schleswig and Holstein. Former is named after town of
Schleswig, known in 804 as Sliesthorp, after bay of Schlei (from Old
Scandinavian sle = 'reed' or perhaps 'channel, canal') on which it is
situated + Old German wik = 'village'; latter was known in 840 as
Holsatia, possibly from German holt = 'wood' + perhaps Old High German sittan = 'to sit' (later taken to be derived from Stein = 'rock').

Scilly Islands (group of islands in North *Atlantic*, south-west of *England*)
Perhaps derived from one rock of group named Scilly, from Irish sceilig
= 'rock', scillic = 'stone splinter' or sceillic = 'rocky islands, sea cliffs'. In

475 BC were known as Tin Islands; tin was not mined here but islands were trading centre for it.

Scotland (north country of *Great Britain*)
Roman name was Caledonia. In 4th–5th centuries Irish Celts called Scots settled here and gave their name to country, with their own name perhaps derived from Celtic scuit = 'to rove, to wander'.

Sebastopol (city and seaport in republic of *Ukraine*, USSR, on south-west coast of *Crimea*)
More correctly, Sevastopol, but derived, when founded in 1783, from Greek sebastos = 'majestic, royal' + polis = 'town'. (For fashion for 'Greek' names in this region at this time see *Odessa*.)

Seine, River (in north *France*, flowing north-west through *Paris* and *Rouen* into English Channel)
Roman name was Sequana, from Celtic soghan = 'calm, quiet' (compare *Saône*). Name gradually changed (Siguna, Signe, Seinne) to present form Seine.

Senegal (republic in West *Africa*)
Named after River Senegal, in turn Portuguese version of name of local tribe (perhaps Berber Zenaga). Has also been explained as deriving from African word = 'navigable'.

Seoul (capital of South *Korea*)
From Chinese form of Korean name of city, Sieur = 'chief town, capital'.

Serbia (province of south-east *Yugoslavia*)
From inhabitants, Serbs, whose own name probably derives from Indo-european serv = 'servant, slave' or perhaps = 'neighbour, ally'.

Severnaya Zemlya (group of islands in *Arctic* Ocean, north of *Siberia*, USSR)
Russian = 'northern land'. Discovered in 1913 by Russian expedition of Vilkitsky and named Nicholas II Islands, after ruling tsar. Named changed to Severnaya Zemlya in 1926.

Seville (province and its capital in south *Spain*)
Probably from Carthaginian sephalas = 'lower', either in sense of 'low-land' or perhaps because situated lower down River *Guadalquivir* than some other town.

Seychelles (group of islands in Indian Ocean, north-east of *Madagascar*)
Discovered by Portuguese in 1504 who named them 'Seven Sisters'. In 1743 islands were captured by French who named them La Bourdonnais, after French governor of *Mauritius*. In 1756 renamed Seychelles after French finance minister, Vicomte de Séchelles.

Shanghai (largest city in *China* and seaport on east coast)
From Chinese = 'on the sea' (Chinese hai = 'sea').

Shannon, River (chief river of *Ireland*, flowing south and west into *Atlantic*)
Ptolemy, writing in 2nd century, referred to it as Senos. Name probably derives from Celtic sen = 'big' + amhan = 'water'. Not likely to be from Old Irish sinda = 'river'.

Shantung (province in east *China* bordering on *Yellow Sea*)
From Chinese shan = 'mountain' + tung = 'east'; ie 'east of the mountain', referring to holy Mount Taishan.

Shenyang (city in *Manchuria*, north-east *China*)
From Chinese yang = 'sunlit river bank' (ie northern, as opposed to ing = 'southern'), + name of River Shen, on which it is situated. Better known by former Manchurian name of *Mukden* = 'height'.

Shetland Islands (north-east of *Orkney Islands*, north of *Scotland*, *Great Britain*)
Settled by Norsemen in 964 and named Hetland, from Old Norse het = 'basalt' (found here). Name later became Shetland.

Siam (former name of *Thailand*)
From Sanskrit sian = 'brown' (referring to colour of skin of natives).

Unlikely to be connected with siamang (type of large gibbon). Name changed to *Thailand* in 1939.

Siberia (region in east USSR, extending from *Urals* to *Pacific*)
Name in 13th century applied to much smaller territory than now. Several possible origins, among which are: 1. related to Russian sever= 'north'; 2. from Mongolian subr = 'mountain wolf'; 3. after Siber, legendary dog who appeared from depths of Lake *Baikal*; 4. from Mongolian shibir = 'marsh'. Last explanation seems most plausible.

Sicily (island south of *Italy*, in *Mediterranean*)
From Siculi (Sekeloi), tribe who inhabited island in 1st century BC, with name probably = 'reapers'.

Sierra Leone (independent state in West *Africa*)
Portuguese explorer Peru de Cintra sighted coast here in 1460 and named it Serra da Leão = 'lion ridge', referring to outline of mountains. Spanish version of name, Sierra Leone, appeared on maps from 1500 with meaning 'lion mountains', perhaps because lions were heard roaring in mountains or referring to roaring sound of wind or sea breaking.

Sierra Madre (mountain system in *Mexico*)
Spanish = 'mother mountains', ie chief mountains of country.

Sierra Nevada (mountain range in east *California*, USA)
Spanish = 'snowy range'. Name was given by Spanish expedition in 1518 to snow-capped mountains, after native Spanish mountains, also named Sierra Nevada. (See also *Nevada*.)

Silesia (region in central east *Europe*, mainly in south-west *Poland*)
Perhaps derived from name of Mount Slenz (present Zobtenberg), religious centre for Vandal tribe of Silingi. Or possibly from Slavonic name of River Slenza, with basic meaning = 'damp'.

Simferopol (city in *Crimea*, south-west USSR, north-east of *Sebastopol*)
So named in 1784, according to prevailing fashion for 'Greek' names (see *Odessa*), from Greek symphero = 'to gather together' or 'to be profitable'

+ polis = 'town'. Earlier name, when city was under Turkish rule, was
Akmechet = 'white mosque'.

Simonstown (town and seaport in South *Africa*, south of *Capetown*)
Named after Dutch Governor of Cape from 1679 to 1699 Simon van
der Stel (compare *Stellenbosch*).

Simplon Pass (through *Alps* in south *Switzerland*)
Named after small village of Simpelen, at south foot of pass, whose own
name derives from Old German words = 'soft height'.

Sinai (peninsula in north-east *Egypt*)
Named after Mount Sinai, from Hebrew sin = 'dirt, mud'.

Singapore (republic, island and city at south extremity of *Malaya*
peninsula, South-East *Asia*)
From Sanskrit singa = 'lion' + pura = 'town'. Name of uncertain origin,
as lions are not native to this region. Perhaps given with sense of 'strong',
or from some personal name. One story tells how Indian prince, arriving
here in 7th century, took the first animal he saw to be a lion.

Skagerrak (strait between *Norway* and *Denmark*, north of *Kattegat*)
In Scandinavian sagas was called Norgeshavet = 'north harbour'. In
16th century Dutch called it Nordzee = 'north sea', and present *Kattegat*—
Skagerrak, from Dutch skagi = 'cape' + rak = 'flowing through a channel'.

Slovakia (eastern part of *Czechoslovakia*, former province)
From name of Slovaks, Slavonic people who inhabited this region. (For
meaning of their name see *Yugoslavia*.)

Slovenia (republic in north-west *Yugoslavia*)
From name of Slovenes, Slavonic people who inhabited this region. (For
meaning of their name see *Yugoslavia*.)

Society Islands in South *Pacific*, east of *Tonga*, French *Polynesia*)
Named by Cook in 1769 in honour of Royal Society in *London* who

were chief instigators of his voyage. Not named after 'society-loving' natives.

Socotra (island in Indian Ocean, north-east of *Somali*, East *Africa*)
From Sanskrit dvina sahadara = 'island of portent of success': island was centrally situated on ancient trade routes from *India* to *Arabia* and *Africa*.

Sofia (capital of *Bulgaria*)
Town of Serdica was built here in 8th–7th centuries BC on site of mineral springs, with name derived from Thracian tribe Serds. Slavs who settled here in 6th century AD took name to mean 'centre' (from Slavonic sered) and called it Sredets. In 11th century after capture by Byzantium renamed Triaditsa, in honour of Holy Trinity. Present name is from Greek = 'wisdom' (used by Byzantium in religious sense) and appeared in 14th century.

Solomon Islands (in South-West *Pacific*, south east of *Bismarck Archipelago*)
Discovered in 1567 by Spanish explorer Alvaro de Mendaña, who seeing gold ornaments worn by natives took islands to be legendary land of Ophir from which, in Bible story (1 Kings 9:28), gold was brought to King Solomon.

Somali (republic in North-East *Africa*)
Probably from Cushite word = 'dark, black' (referring to colour of skin of natives).

Somme, River (in north *France* flowing west into English Channel)
In Caesar's time was Samara, possibly from Indoeuropean sai = 'to flow' + ar = 'water'; could also be connected with Celtic soghar = 'quiet' (compare *Seine*, *Saône*).

Soviet Union (official name of *Russia*)
Name first officially used in 1922 when, after 1917 Revolution, new constitution of socialist republics was set up with soviet (Russian = 'council') as basic unit of local and national government.

Spain (state in south-west *Europe* on Iberian Peninsula)
Carthaginians, who set up colonies on shores here, named country Span =
'rabbit' (because animal was abundant here). But this may have been
attempt to explain Basque ezpaña = 'shore', or to give meaning to the
name of some Iberian tribe. Roman name was Hispania, from which
derives modern Spain.

Spencer Gulf (inlet of Indian Ocean in coast of South *Australia*)
Discovered by Matthew Flinders in 1802 and named after English Earl
Spencer, First Lord of Admiralty at time voyage of Flinders was com-
missioned.

Spitzbergen (group of islands in *Arctic* Ocean, north of *Norway*)
Russian coastal dwellers of 15th century knew islands as Grumant, from
Swedish Grönland = 'green land'. Name Spitzbergen derives from
Dutch spits = 'point' + bergen = 'mountains' and was given by Dutch
explorer Barents who landed on islands in 1596. Scandinavian name is
Svalbard = 'cold country'.

Split (town and seaport on *Adriatic*, west *Yugoslavia*)
Original Palatium = 'palace' (compare modern Italian name Spalato).
In 740 inhabitants built their houses on walls of restored palace of Diocletian, which in 78 BC had been place of refuge (stronghold) of population.

Springfield (state capital of *Illinois*, USA)
Common name in USA, usually denoting place grown up round a
spring or some water-source. The 1st name of Springfield was given in
1641 to town in *Massachusetts* by English settler William Pynchon after
village of Springfield in Essex; other towns, including capital of *Illinois*,
derived from this (with exception of Springfield, South *Carolina*, which
is named after man called Spring).

Sri Lanka (island republic off south-east coast of *India*)
From native (Sinhalese) = 'blessed island'. Tibetan name of island is
Langka (Sanskrit lanka = 'island'). Until 1972 name was *Ceylon*.

Stanley Falls (on River *Congo*, *Zaire*, Central *Africa*)
Named after English explorer H. M. Stanley (real name John Rowlands), who discovered them in 1877.

Stellenbosch (town in *Cape Province*, South *Africa*, east of *Capetown*)
Founded in 1679 by Dutch coloniser Simon van der Stel (compare *Simonstown*) + bosch = 'wood'. Town is oldest in South Africa after *Capetown*.

Stockholm (capital of *Sweden*)
2nd element is from Swedish holm = 'island'; 1st element is of doubtful origin: perhaps from stäk = 'bay' or stock = 'post, pole' (referring to landmark or remains of some building).

Strasbourg (city in *Alsace*, north-east *France*)
From German Strasse = 'street, road' + Burg = 'town', ie 'town by the road' (leading from River *Rhine* over *Vosges* to the west).

Stromboli (volcanic island north of *Sicily*, in *Tyrrhenian Sea*)
From Greek strongylos = 'round' (referring to shape of volcano).

Stuttgart (city in south-west of West *Germany*)
Recorded in 1229 as Stutengarten, literally = 'mare's garden' (from German Stute = 'mare' + Garten = 'garden'), from horse-breeding carried on here.

Sudan (republic in North-East *Africa*)
From Arabic bilyad-es-sudan = 'country of the black' (ie land of Negroes)

Suez (gulf forming north-west arm of *Red Sea*, linked with *Mediterranean* by Suez Canal)
Possibly connected with Egyptian suan = 'beginning' (ie situated at 'beginning' of *Red Sea*).

Sumatra (island in *Indonesia*, south-west of *Malaya*)
Name known in this form since 1390; perhaps from Sanskrit samudra = 'ocean', but origin not really certain.

Superior, Lake (largest of Great Lakes between *Canada* and USA)
In sense of 'upper, higher' (upstream from other Great Lakes); flows into
Lake *Huron* and Lake *Michigan*.

Swaziland (kingdom in South-East *Africa*, bordered on three sides by
Transvaal)
Named after Bantus tribe, Swazis, related to Zulus; their name may
derive from that of their chief, Swazi, perhaps = 'rod'.

Sweden (kingdom in north *Europe*)
From Swedish Svea-rike = 'kingdom of the Svea (Suiones)', Germanic
people who with the Goths once inhabited south *Sweden*. Their name
comes from Old High German geswion = 'kinsman'.

Switzerland (republic in west *Europe*)
Named after canton Schwyz, with its own name perhaps connected
with Old High German suedan = 'to burn' (ie territory where forest was
cleared by burning).

Sydney (largest city in *Australia*, capital of *New South Wales*)
Founded as 1st English colony in 1788 and named after English Secretary
of State Lord Sydney

Syracuse (city on south-east coast of *Sicily*, south *Italy*)
First Greek colony on the island. Name is of pre-Greek origin, of uncertain meaning, but perhaps from Phoenician serach = 'to stink' (town
was built by swamp). Name was transferred to American town of Syracuse in *New York* state in 1825.

Syria (republic in South-West *Asia*, south of *Turkey*)
Of uncertain origin, though country called Suri in Asia Minor is mentioned in Babylonian cuneiform script of about 4000 BC. Not likely to
be Greek abbreviation of *Assyria*.

T

Table Mountain (in *Cape Province*, South *Africa*)
So named in 1503 by Portuguese navigator Antonio de Saldanha, who
was struck by appearance of flat top of mountain with white cloud hanging over it like a cloth.

Tadjikistan (republic in south central USSR, north of *Afghanistan*)
Named after inhabitants, Tadzhiks (+ Iranian stan = 'country'), whose
name may derive from word = 'wreathed' (referring to national headdress), or from Old Persian tachik = 'Arab' (because of Moslem faith).

Tagus, River (rising in east *Spain* and flowing west through *Portugal*
into *Atlantic*)
Name is of Iberian origin, of unknown meaning; perhaps from Latin
tagus = 'ravine, canyon'.

Tahiti (largest island in French *Polynesia*, South *Pacific*, one of *Society
Islands*)
Earlier name was Hiti-nui, from Polynesian nui = 'island', perhaps with
1st element derived from iti = 'small island'. Name changed later to
Hitiiti, then to Tahiti.

Taiwan (island off south-east coast of *China*)
From Chinese = 'terraced shore' (referring to appearance of highlands,
foothills and sandy beaches descending as a 'terrace'). Earlier (Portuguese)
name was *Formosa*.

Talien (part of Chinese port of *Lü-ta*)
Chinese variant of Russian name *Dairen*, in turn a variant of *Dalny*.

Tallahassee (state capital of *Florida*, USA)
From Indian (Muskogean) word = 'old town'.

Tallinn (capital of republic of *Estonia*, north-west USSR)
From Estonian taani = 'Danes' + linna = 'town'; territory was ruled by
Danes from 1227 to 1346. Name before 1917 was Revel, of uncertain
meaning: perhaps connected with Danish revele = 'sandbank'.

Tananarive (capital of *Malagasy Republic*)
Probably from Malagasy word = 'thousand villages' (from tanana = 'village'). Element -riv occurs many times on island, probably indicating passage of Malayan settlers from east coast.

Tanganyika (former name of chief part of present *Tanzania*, East *Africa*, and lake here)
English explorer Burton, who discovered lake in 1858, explained name as deriving from kou tanganyika = 'to join, to meet' (ie 'place where waters meet'). Stanley, on the other hand, explained it as coming from tonga = 'island' + hika = 'plain'. In many Bantu languages -nyika = 'plain'. Lake gave name to country.

Tangier (seaport on north coast of *Morocco*, North-West *Africa*)
Perhaps connected with Berber andji = 'river', but Carthaginian name was Tingis, from Semitic tigisis = 'harbour', and this could have evolved into modern name Tangier.

Tanzania (republic in central East *Africa*)
From 1st elements of *Tanganyika* and *Zanzibar* + Latin-type ending -ia denoting territory. Two countries united to form Tanzania in 1964.

Taranto (city and seaport in *Apulia*, south-east *Italy*)
Founded in 8th century BC by emigrants from *Greece*. Name may derive from Illyrian darandos = 'oak'.

Tashkent (capital of republic of *Uzbekistan*, USSR)
Probably from Turkish tash = 'stone' + Iranian kent = 'town'.

Tasmania (island south of *Australia*)
Named in 1853 after Dutch navigator Abel Tasman (1603–59) who was the first European to sight it, in 1642. He named it Van Diemen's Land, after Dutch admiral Anthony van Diemen, governor general of Dutch settlements in East Indies.

Tbilisi (capital of republic of *Georgia*, USSR)
From Georgian tbili = 'warm' (referring to mineral springs here). Before 1935 was known as Tiflis, corruption of Tbilisi.

Tehran (capital of *Iran*)
Probably = 'plain', as distinct from Shamran, with name = 'mountain district', which lies to north-west of Tehran. Or possibly = 'pure, beautiful'.

Tel Aviv (largest city in *Israel*, on *Mediterranean* north-west of *Jerusalem*)
Hebrew = 'hill of spring' (tel = 'hill'). City was founded in 1909 near *Jaffa*, with which it amalgamated in 1949.

Tenerife (largest of *Canary Islands*, off north-west coast of *Africa*)
Roman name was Nivaria, from Latin nix, nivis = 'snow'. Name of Tenerife was recorded in 16th century with meaning 'white mountain'.

Tennessee (state in central south USA)
Named after River Tennessee, tributary of River *Ohio*, from Indian (Cherokee) Tenn-assee, perhaps name of tribe = 'crooked ears', or with simple meaning 'river'.

Texas (state in south-west USA)
True origin unknown. Story is that Spanish monk Damian, landing on coast here in 1690, asked Indians to which tribe they belonged, receiving reply 'texia' (= 'good friend'—their form of greeting). But this could have been tribal name.

Thailand (kingdom in South-East *Asia*, north of *Malaya*)
From native name Tyang-tai = 'country of the free'. Name before 1939 was *Siam*.

Thames, River (chief river of *England* flowing east through *London* into *North Sea*)
Julius Caesar wrote of it in 51 BC as Tamesis (last element of which is said to give name of river at and above Oxford—Isis). Perhaps derives

from Celtic tam = 'widening' + isis = 'water', or from Indoeuropean root word ta = 'to flow'.

Tiber, River (in *Italy* rising in *Apennines* and flowing south through *Rome* into *Tyrrhenian Sea*)
From Roman name Tiberis, perhaps derived from Celtic dubr = 'water'.

Tibet (autonomous region in south-west *China*)
Of uncertain origin. Perhaps connected with Tibetan thub = 'strong, powerful'. Original name was Tu-pho, possibly corrupted by Arabs into Tibat.

Tientsin (3rd largest city in *China*, south-east of *Peking*)
Of uncertain meaning. Has been explained as deriving from Chinese tyang = 'heaven' + tsin = 'entrance, gates', but 1st word means both 'heaven' and 'day' so that meaning could be 'day ford'.

Tierra del Fuego (group of islands at south extremity of South *America*, divided between *Chile* and *Argentina*)
Spanish = 'land of fire'. On his 1st journey round the world in 1520 Magellan sighted fires here, either bonfires or on moving boats, and so named islands thus.

Tigris, River (in South-West *Asia*, rising in east *Turkey* and flowing south-east through *Iraq* to join *Euphrates* and enter Persian Gulf)
In cuneiform was named as Indigna, and later as Dignat. Sumerian name was Tig-ru-shu, from tig = 'spear' + ru = 'to overthrow' + shu = 'to capture', ie 'running with an overthrowing (conquering) spear'. Sanskrit name Tigris was connected with Old Persian tigra = 'arrow', perhaps in sense of 'fast-flowing' (in contrast to River *Euphrates*).

Timor (island in Malay Archipelago, politically divided between *Indonesia* and *Portugal*)
From Indonesian word = 'east'. Island is most easterly of Lesser Sunda Islands.

Tirana (capital of *Albania*)
Origin has been explained as name given by Turkish pasha Suleiman, who when founding city about 1600 called it Tigran after his native Teheran (*Tehran*). But a Venetian document of 1572 mentions settlement here as 'il borgo di Tirana' (= 'the village of Tirana'). Tirania was ancient name of *Tuscany*, and so connected with the Tuscans, an Albanian people (south *Albania* was known as Toscenia). (See also *Tyrrhenian Sea*.)

Titicaca, Lake (largest lake in South *America*, divided between *Peru* and *Bolivia*)
Name derives from island on lake, whose name perhaps = 'sunny island' or 'lead mountain'.

Titograd (capital of *Montenegro*, *Yugoslavia*)
Named in 1948 in honour of Marshal Tito, President of *Yugoslavia* from 1953, + Slavonic grad = 'town'. Earlier name was Podgorica = 'under the mountain'.

Tobago (island in *West Indies*, north-east of *Trinidad*)
Discovered by Columbus in 1498, who named it Tobago from Haitian tambaku = 'pipe' (used by natives for smoking tobacco, which word also derives from it).

Tobruk (seaport in *Libya*, east of *Benghazi*)
Greek name was Antipirgos = 'opposite the tower' (bay was protected from the wind by an island opposite which, on the beach, was a tower). Present name is probably Arabic corruption of Greek name.

Togo (republic in West *Africa*, on Gulf of *Guinea*)
Named after Lake Togo, with name of unknown origin.

Tokyo (capital of *Japan*)
From Japanese to = 'east' + kio = 'capital' (as distinct from Kyoto, = 'western capital', which it replaced as capital in 1869).

Toledo (province and its capital in central *Spain*, south of *Madrid*)
From Celtic tol = 'mountain' (town stands on hill of granite). (Compare
Toulon, Toulouse.)

Tonga (group of islands in South *Pacific*, south-east of *Fiji*)
Native name for main island is Tonga, or Tongatabu, = 'holy'. Name was
spread by Dutch explorers, who discovered it in 1616, to whole group.
Cook named group *Friendly Islands*.

Tonkin (former French protectorate in north Indo-China, present North
Vietnam)
From Chinese tong = 'eastern' + kin = 'capital'; name originally applied
to *Hanoi*, but later spread to whole country. Tonkin was under Chinese
rule until 1802, and from 1950 became part of *Vietnam*.

Topeka (state capital of *Kansas*, USA)
From Indian (Sioux) word = 'potato good place' (ie where wild tuber,
which English called potato, was dug up by natives).

Toronto (capital of *Ontario*, 2nd largest city in *Canada*)
Founded in 1794 with name of York, in honour of Duke of York, son
of English king George III, on site of Indian settlement named Toronto,
perhaps derived from Iroquois Toron-to-hen = 'timber in the water', or
from similar Indian words = 'place of assembly' or 'place of plenty'.
Toronto became official name of city from 1834.

Torrens, Lake (in state of South *Australia*)
Named after English economist and soldier, Colonel Robert Torrens
(1780–1864), one of founders of colony of South *Australia* in 1834.

Torres Strait (between New *Guinea* and Cape *York, Queensland*, north
Australia)
Named in 1769 in memory of Spanish navigator Luis Torres, who discovered the strait in 1606 when sailing west from *Pacific* towards *Indonesia*.

Tortuga (island north-west of *Haiti, West Indies*)
Spanish = 'turtle'. Name given by Columbus in 1492, with reference to many turtles found here.

Toulon (city and seaport in south *France*, south-east of *Marseilles*)
Greek name was Telonion. Name is pre-Gaulish and very ancient. May be of Ligurian origin with lost meaning, from unknown Phoenician word, or from pre-Indoeuropean word based on t-l = 'mountain', passed down to Celts in form tul or tol (compare *Toledo*).

Toulouse (city in south-west *France*, on River *Garonne*)
Possibly from Celtic tul = 'mountain', or Iberian (pre-Latin) word of unknown meaning.

Touraine (historic province in west central *France*)
From name of its inhabitants, Turoni, Gaulish tribe with name probably derived from Celtic tur = 'water'. (See also *Tours*, its capital.)

Tours (city in west central *France*, south-west of *Paris*)
Former capital of *Touraine*; Roman name was Civitas Turonum = 'town of the Turoni'. Official name—Caesarodunum = 'Caesar's city' (from Gaulish dun = 'town')—did not last and by 3rd century had fallen out of use.

Trabzon (town and port on *Black Sea*, north-east *Turkey*)
Dispute about origin of name has lasted over 2000 years. Could derive from Greek trapeza = 'table', referring to shape of nearby mountain. (Many mountains on *Black Sea* coast are called 'Table' from their flat top.) Or could be connected with geometrical figure trapezium. The 3rd theory is that immigrants from town of Trapezos in Arcadia (ancient Greek province) colonised Trabzon and named it after their native town (in turn probably derived from a personal name).

Trafalgar, Cape (in south *Spain* between *Cadiz* and *Gibraltar*)
From Arabic Tarf-el-garb = 'western point' (Arabic tarf = 'point, sand, earth' + el garb = 'the west'). Or possibly from Arabic taraf-al-aghar = 'pillar-cave', referring to one of pillars of Hercules in Greek mythology.

Transvaal (province in north-east of South *Africa*)
From Latin trans = 'across' + name of River *Vaal*. Name arose in 1830s when Boers from Cape Colony retreated north-east from English troops to other side of River *Vaal*.

Transylvania (former province in north-west *Romania*)
From Latin trans = 'across' + silva = 'forest', ie 'land beyond the forest'.

Trebizond (former name of *Trabzon*)

Trenton (state capital of *New Jersey*, USA)
Originally was Trent's Town, after name of founder in early 18th century, William Trent.

Trieste (seaport in north-east *Italy*, on *Adriatic Sea*)
Recorded by Pliny as Tergeste. May derive from Illyrian terga = 'trade', or terst = 'reed'.

Trinidad (island in *West Indies*, off north-west coast of *Venezuela*)
Discovered by Columbus in 1498, perhaps on Trinity Sunday, after which day he named it (Spanish trinidad = 'trinity'), but more likely because of 3 peaks he saw as he approached.

Tripoli (joint capital with *Benghazi*, of *Libya*, North *Africa*)
From Greek tripolis = 'three towns', ie ancient cities of Osa, Sabratha and Leptis. (Tripoli in *Lebanon* has same origin, referring to Tyre, Sidon and Aradus.)

Tristan da Cunha (group of islands in South *Atlantic*, south-west of South *Africa*)
Named after Portuguese explorer who discovered them in 1506.

Trucial States (former name of *United Arab Emirates*)
So named from agreement made with *Britain* in 1820 to ensure condition of truce in territory, once known as the Pirate Coast. Became *United Arab Emirates* in 1971 (for names of states see this).

Tuamotu (group of islands in French *Polynesia* (*Oceania*), South *Pacific*, east of *Society Islands*)
From native name Puamotu = 'distant islands', probably given by inhabitants of *Tahiti*. Also known as Low Islands, Pearl Islands, Dangerous Islands, all self-explanatory names.

Tunisia (republic in North-West *Africa*, with capital Tunis)
Country named after its capital, with name falsely connected with Phoenician goddess Tanith. City was known in pre-Phoenician times, and was mentioned by Greek historians Polybius and Diodorus, writing in 1st century BC. Exact origin still uncertain.

Turin (4th largest city in *Italy*, in north-west on River *Po*)
Region was inhabited by Ligurian tribe Taurini, with name perhaps connected with Celtic tur = 'water'. Roman name of city was Augusta Taurinorum, after Emperor Augustus.

Turkestan (region in Central *Asia*, partly in USSR, partly in *China*)
Name is of Iranian origin = 'country of the Turks' (Iranian stan = 'country').

Turkey (republic in South-West *Asia*, with small area in south-east *Europe*)
Named after inhabitants, Turks, + ending -ey = Latin suffix -ia denoting territory. Name of people is probably derived from tora = 'to be born', or perhaps connected with English 'turban', their headdress.

Turkmenistan (republic in south USSR bordering on *Iran*)
Named after Turkmens, who form bulk of population, + Iranian stan = 'country'. Name of people is of doubtful origin, possibly from turkmend = 'Turk-like'—though 'men' in Turkish languages has many meanings and native name has been variously interpreted as 'pure Turks', 'good Turks', 'great Turks', etc.

Turks Islands (in *West Indies*, north of *Hispaniola*, east of Caicos Islands)
Said to derive from local cactus known as Turk's head, from its shape.

Turku (3rd largest city in *Finland*, on Gulf of *Bothnia*, north-west of *Helsinki*)
From Finnish turku = 'trading place, market square', word borrowed from Old Russian torg = 'trade'. For long time official name of town was Åbo, from Swedish, deriving from Indoeuropean word = 'water'.

Tuscany (region in central *Italy* bordering on Ligurian and *Tyrrhenian* Seas)
Named after Etruscans (Tuscans), who inhabited region here 1000 BC. Their name is of unknown origin. (See also *Tyrrhenian Sea*.)

Tyrol (province in west *Austria*)
Medieval Latin name was Castrum Terolis = 'fort of Terol', in turn from ancient fortress of Teriolis, recorded about 400 BC, whose name has been preserved in small town of Zirl near *Innsbruck*. Or perhaps from Celtic tir = 'land'.

Tyrrhenian Sea (part of *Mediterranean* between south *Italy* and *Sardinia* and *Sicily*)
From Greek name for Etruscans—Tyrrhenoi—who inhabited BC region that is now *Tuscany*.

J **Uganda** (republic in East *Africa*)
Name derives from province of *Buganda*; Uganda is Swahili form, used along east coast.

Ukraine (republic in south-west USSR, bordering on *Black Sea*)
Name = 'border territory', from Slavonic root krai = 'boundary, frontier'. After Tatar invasion of 13th century and that of Poles and Lithuanians in 14th century many peasants fled to unpopulated area along River *Dnieper* and set up a 'border territory'.

Ulan Bator (capital of *Mongolia*)
Until 1924 was Urga, Mongolian = 'abode' or 'palace'. Renamed Ulan Bator, from Mongolian ulan = 'red' + bator = 'warrior', in honour of

Suhe-Bator (1893-1923) who founded modern republic of *Mongolia* in 1911 and who was born near Urga.

Ulm (town in south of West *Germany*, south-east of *Stuttgart*)
Probably of Celtic origin, with basic meaning = 'marshy', or possibly from Germanic word of similar meaning (Low German ulm = 'decay', Norwegian dialect word ulma = 'mould').

Ulster (alternative name for Northern *Ireland*)
From ancient tribal name Ulaid, in turn from Irish uladh = 'dwelling-towns', + Old Norse stathr = 'place'.

Umbria (region in central *Italy*, in *Apennines*)
From Umbrians, Roman people who inhabited this region BC, with their own name derived from Indoeuropean root word = 'water-dwellers'.

United Arab Emirates (union of 6 states on south coast of Persian Gulf, bordering on *Saudi Arabia*, and one on Gulf of *Oman*)
Until 1971 was *Trucial States*, when formed independent state of 7 emirates of Abu Dhabi, Ajman, Dubai, Fujairah (which joined state in 1972), Ras al Khaimah, Sharjah and Umm al Qaiwain.

Urals (mountains running from north to south in USSR and forming natural frontier between *Europe* and *Asia*)
Perhaps from Tatar ural = 'girdle', in sense of 'belt' between East and West, or connected with name of *Aral Sea* (from whose depths, according to legend, mountains came) with meaning 'island', in sense of mountains rising like islands from surrounding flat country.

Uruguay (republic in South *America*)
Named after River Uruguay (tributary of River *Plate*) with origin perhaps in Indian guay = 'tail' + uru = 'bird', referring to species of bird with remarkable tail living in forests here. Or perhaps connected with guay = 'river', common element in South *American* names.

Ushant (island off west coast of *Brittany*, *France*)
French name is Ouessant, falsely connected with French ouest = 'west'.

Name is in fact derived from Roman Axantos or Uxantis Insula, from Gaulish ux = 'high' + ending denoting superlative.

Utah (state in west USA)
From name of Indian tribe Ute = 'tall' (either literally, or in sense of living in mountains).

Utrecht (city in central *Netherlands*, south-east of *Amsterdam*)
In 723 was Roman Trajectum castrum = 'camp crossing' (ie 'camp by the crossing'). In 10th century name had been shortened to Trecht, but in 11th–12th centuries appeared in modern form Utrecht (with Dutch prefix ut = 'lower'), first applying to (lower) suburbs, then to whole town.

Uttar Pradesh (state in north *India*)
Sanskrit = 'northern province'. Present name was adopted in 1950; before this (from 1902) name was United Provinces of Agra and Oudh.

Uzbekistan (republic in south USSR, bordering in south on *Afghanistan*)
Named after inhabitants, Uzbeks, + Iranian stan = 'country'. Name of people said to derive from Khan Uzbek, chief of Golden Horde in 14th century, though Uzbek language and race existed before this.

Vaal, River (in South *Africa*, rising in *Transvaal* and flowing south-west into *Cape Province* to join River Orange)
Name was given by Boers (Dutch colonisers), from Dutch vaal = 'grey, murky', possibly translation of Hottentot ki-garep = 'yellow'.

Valencia (region and historic province in east *Spain*)
Founded by Romans in 137 BC with name Valencia Edetanorum = 'stronghold of the Edenti'; 1st word has survived to give modern name of city of Valencia.

Valenciennes (town in north-east *France* on River *Scheldt*, south-east of *Lille*)
Name arose during period of Roman occupation, from Latin Valen-

tinianae, later Valentiana, after Roman emperor Valentinian I (ruled AD 364–75).

Valladolid (city in *Spain*, north-west of *Madrid*)
From Spanish valle = 'valley' + Olid, possibly personal name of founder or ruler.

Valletta (capital of *Malta*)
Named after Jean de la Valette, Grand Master of the Knights of Malta, who founded city in 1565 after victory over Turks.

Valparaiso (city and seaport in *Chile*, South *America*, north-west of *Santiago*)
Founded by Spanish explorer Juan de Saavedra in 1536 with name = 'valley of paradise' (Spanish valle paraiso), because of beauty and fertility of region.

Vancouver (city, seaport and island on *Pacific* in west *Canada*)
Named, as is Vancouver, *Washington*, USA, after English explorer George Vancouver (1758–98), who surveyed Vancouver Island in 1792 as midshipman in Cook's last expedition.

Varanasi (official name of *Benares, India*)

Varna (city, seaport and resort on *Black Sea*, *Bulgaria*, south-east of *Sofia*)
Possibly from Slavonic voron = 'raven' (perhaps in sense of 'black' as situated on *Black Sea*), or perhaps from Indoeuropean var = 'water'.

Vatican (papal state in *Rome, Italy*)
From Latin name of hill on which it stands, Mons Vaticanus, in turn perhaps from vaticinia = 'place of divination' (ie a pagan shrine).

Venezuela (republic in South *America*, on *Caribbean Sea*)
Spanish explorers discovered here in 1499, on shores of Lake *Maracaibo*, an Indian village built on piles. This reminded them of *Venice*, so they

named it Venezuela = 'little Venice'. Name subsequently spread to surrounding territory and in 1830 became official name of country.

Venice (city and seaport on *Adriatic Sea*, north-east *Italy*)
In 5th century BC territory here was inhabited by Illyrian tribe Veneti, whose own name probably derives from Indoeuropean venis = 'friend' (in sense of 'one of us'). Romans named territory after tribe, and name then passed to town which arose here in AD 451 out of an 'amalgamation' of fishing villages on the various islands.

Veracruz (state and seaport in *Mexico*, on Gulf of *Mexico*)
Spanish soldier Cortez founded town here in Holy Week, 1519, and named it Villa rica de la Vera Cruz = 'rich town of the true cross', in commemoration of Crucifixion.

Verdun (town in east *France* on River *Meuse*, west of *Metz*)
From Celtic dun = 'mountain' or 'fort', with doubtful 1st element. Name perhaps meant something like 'defensive dam on the river (*Meuse*)'.

Vereeniging (town in *Transvaal*, South *Africa*, on River *Vaal*)
Dutch = 'association'. Town was founded in 1892 and named after original owners, Suid Afrikaanse en Oranje Vrijstaatse Kolen en Mineralen Myn Vereeniging = 'South African and Orange Free State Coal and Mineral Mining Association'. Name does not refer to attempts at political union between South African Republic and *Orange Free State*.

Vermont (state in *New England*, north-east USA)
From French vert mont (correctly, mont vert) = 'green mountain', a rendering by Dr Thomas Young of earlier English name Green Mountain.

Verona (city in north *Italy*, north of *Venice*)
Ancient name was Vernomagos, from Celtic vernos = 'alder-tree' + magos = 'field'.

Versailles (town with famous palace of Versailles, south-west of *Paris*, *France*)
From Latin versus = 'slope' + ending -alia.

Vesuvius (volcano in *Campania*, south *Italy*, south-east of *Naples*)
From Oscan fesf = 'smoke' (compare *Etna*).

Vichy (resort and spa in central *France*)
From Roman name Vicus calidus = 'warm place', referring to warm springs for which town is famous.

Victoria (1. state in South-East *Australia*; 2. capital of British *Columbia*; 3. lake, otherwise Nyanza, in East *Africa*; 4. falls on River *Zambezi* on *Zambia–Rhodesia* frontier; 5. island in *Arctic* Ocean, north *Canada*; 6. land in *Ross Dependency*, *Antarctic*)
All named after English queen Victoria (reigned 1837–1901); all once part of British empire; all either discovered or founded and named during her reign.

Vienna (capital of *Austria*)
Named after River Vienna, which at this point flows into River *Danube*. Name of river probably derives from Celtic vedunia = 'tree', or perhaps from Celtic vindo = 'white', 'building'.

Vietnam (country in South-East *Asia*, south of *China*, politically divided into North and South)
From Annamese = 'land of the south'. Before 1945 was Annam, *Tonkin* and part of *Cochin-China*.

Vilnius (capital of republic of *Lithuania*, north-west USSR)
From River Viliya (or Nyaris) on which it stands. Name of river probably derives from Baltic-Slavonic word = 'winding'.

Virgin Islands (in *West Indies*, east of *Puerto Rico*)
Discovered by Columbus in 1493, who is said to have named them after feast-day of St Ursula and the Virgin Martyrs (21 October) on which day he sighted them. But some of the islands were probably in-

cluded in grant of English king Charles I to Earl of Carlisle in 1627 and may then have been named in honour of Elizabeth I (1533–1603), the 'Virgin Queen'. (See also *Virginia*.)

Virginia (state in central east USA, bordering on *Atlantic*)
Founded by English settlers in 1607 and named in honour of Elizabeth I (reigned 1558–1603), the 'Virgin Queen'. In American Civil War of 1861–5 state was divided into North and South, as a result of which state of West *Virginia* was formed. Name may originally have also had suggestion of 'virgin land', ripe for settlement.

Vistula, River (rising in *Carpathians* and flowing west and north-west through *Poland* into *Baltic Sea*)
Of uncertain origin. Possibly from Slavonic word derived from Indo-european veis = 'to flow', which explanation is supported by west Slavonic dialect word visla = 'river, stream' (Polish name of river is Wisla). But even Celtic origin has been suggested, with connection with Irish uisge = 'water'.

Vladimir (city in west USSR, east of *Moscow*)
Founded as a fortress at beginning of 12th century, and named after prince who founded it, Vladimir Monomakh.

Vladivostok (city and seaport in east USSR on Sea of *Japan*)
Founded in 1860 with name modelled on that of Vladikavkaz (founded 1784), with meaning 'eastern possession' (Russian vladenie = 'possession' + vostok = 'east'). (Vladikavkaz = 'possession of the *Caucasus*'.)

Volga, River (longest river in *Europe*, in west USSR, flowing east and south into *Caspian Sea*)
Many possible meanings, none of them certain. More likely derivations are: 1. from Slavonic vlaga = 'damp, moisture'; 2. from Estonian valge, Finnish valkea = 'white, bright'; 3. from Old Slavonic volkoi, Russian veliki = 'great'.

Volgograd (city in south-west USSR on River *Volga*)
Slavonic = 'Volga town'. Until 1961 was Stalingrad (= 'Stalin's town').

Until 1925, from foundation in about 1589, was Tsaritsyn, not from Russian tsaritsa (tsar's wife) but from Turkish sarygshin = 'yellowish' (referring to colour of water of River *Volga*).

Volta, River (in central West *Africa* flowing south-east through republic of Upper Volta and *Ghana* into Gulf of *Guinea*)
Name was given by Portuguese explorers and first appeared on map of 1741 as Rio de volta = 'river of return', ie river by which expedition returned.

Vosges (mountains and department in east *France*)
From Celtic vos = 'peak'.

Walachia (region in south *Romania*)
From inhabitants, Walachians or Vlachs, non-Slavonic people with name = 'foreigner' and corresponding to Welsh of *Wales* and Walloons of south *Belgium* and north-east *France*, none of whom are native to chief surrounding country. (See also *Walcheren*.)

Walcheren (island in estuary of River *Scheldt, Netherlands*)
Name in 7th century was Walacria; main element is Germanic walh = 'foreigner', referring to inhabitants who were of non-Germanic origin. (See *Walachia, Wales*.)

Wales (principality in south-west *Great Britain*)
Latin name was Cambria, from native inhabitants, Cymry (= Celts). Name Wales was probably given by Anglo-Saxons, who invaded *Britain* in 5th–6th centuries, from Old English wealh = 'foreigner' (in sense of people who were of different stock to themselves and who would not assimilate with them). (See also *Walachia, Walcheren*.)

Warsaw (capital of *Poland*)
Many (unlikely) stories regarding origin, eg named after twins War and Sawa, found by king out hunting; from cry of raftsmen on River *Vistula* to their cook, 'Warz, Eva!' (Polish = 'Broth, Eve!'). Possibly derived from rich Czech family named Warsew who founded city in 11th cen-

tury or perhaps from Hungarian varos = 'fortified town'. Most likely to be derived from name of founder Warsz, + ending -ev = 'belonging to'. Polish name of city is Warszawa.

Washington (1. capital of USA in District of *Columbia*; 2. state in extreme north-west USA)
Capital was founded in 1791 and named after George Washington (1732–99), 1st president of the USA. State was founded in 1853 and was nearly named Columbia, but at last moment one of members of Congress proposed name Washington, also in honour of president. Objections that state and capital might be confused were overruled as being 'unpatriotic'.

Waterloo (small town in province of *Brabant, Belgium*, south of *Brussels*)
Flemish = 'watery marsh'; but there is no marsh nearby so 2nd element may derive not from Flemish loo = 'marsh' but from Old High German loh = 'wood', or, more likely, from Old High German losi = 'ditch', element often combined with word water.

Weddell Sea (in *Antarctic*, in British Antarctic Territory)
Named in 1823 after English seal-hunter Robert Weddell.

Weimar (town in south-west of East *Germany*, south-west of *Leipzig*)
From Old High German win = 'meadow, pasture', or wih = 'holy', + mari = 'standing water, lake'.

Wellington (capital of *New Zealand* and its province, at south end of North Island)
City founded in 1840 and named in honour of English soldier and statesman Duke of Wellington (1769–1852). Province named after city. (Capital before 1865 was *Auckland*.)

Weser, River (in north of West *Germany* flowing north into *North Sea*)
Old German name was Wisuraha, possibly connected with Indoeuropean wis-ko-s = 'running water' (or with German Wasser = 'water').

West Indies (large group of islands off Central *America*, separating *Atlantic* from *Caribbean Sea*)

Discovered by Columbus in 1492–1504 and so named by him in error, in the belief that he had reached *India* by a western route.

Westphalia (former province in north-west of West *Germany*, originally west part of *Saxony*)
Named after Westphalians (= 'western Phalians'), as distinct from Ost-phalians ('eastern Phalians'), Germanic tribe inhabiting territory in time of Charlemagne. The 2nd element of name derives from Old High German falaho = 'field-dweller'.

White Russia (English name for *Byelorussia*)
Translation of name, from Russian byely = 'white' + Russia.

White Sea (inlet of *Barents Sea*, north-west USSR)
Probably so named from colour of water reflecting snowy *Arctic* sky, or from snow-covered ice of sea in winter, but could also = 'north' according to ancient system of naming parts of world by colour (compare *Black Sea*).

Wiesbaden (city in central West *Germany*, west of *Frankfurt*)
In 1st–2nd centuries had Latin name Aquae Mattiacae = 'waters of Mat-tiacus'. In 830 was Uisibada, with element bad also = 'waters' (ie mineral waters), but with 1st element uisi of doubtful origin—perhaps connected with German Wies = 'meadow'.

Wight, Isle of (in south *England*, in English Channel)
Latin name was Vectis, corrupted to modern Wight. Meaning 'white' (referring to chalk cliffs) is attempt to 'translate' Latin name, which itself is of uncertain origin, though could = 'lever', in sense of 'land that has been pushed up out of the sea'.

Wilhelmshaven (city and seaport in north-east of West *Germany*, north-west of *Bremen*)
Naval base was established here in 1853 and named Wilhelmshaven (= 'Wilhelm's harbour') in honour of German emperor Wilhelm I.

Wilkes Land (territory in Australian Antarctic Territory)
First sighted by American explorer Charles Wilkes in 1839.

Windhoek (capital of South-West *Africa*)
Dutch = 'windy cape', so named from prevailing south-east winds. Was
called Windhuk when capital of German South-West *Africa* (1892–1915).

Windward Islands (in *West Indies*, south of *Leeward Islands*)
Located in path of north-east Trade Winds (unlike *Leeward Islands*, which
are sheltered from them).

Winnipeg (capital and largest city of *Manitoba, Canada*, and lake in this
province)
City is named after lake, in turn from Indian (Cree) vinipi = 'muddy
water'. Original name of city when founded in 1738 was Fort Rouge
(French = 'red fort'), as it stood on Red River. Name was then changed
twice: to Fort Douglas, after family name of Lord Selkirk, who established Scottish colony here, and to Fort Garry, after one of officers of
Hudson Bay Company. Eventually became Winnipeg in 1873.

Wisconsin (state in north USA, bordering on Lake *Superior* and Lake
Michigan)
Named after River Wisconsin, in turn probably French variant of Indian
(Algonquian) name of uncertain meaning, perhaps = 'big long river',
'grassy plain' or 'river of a thousand islands'. State officially adopted name
in 1783.

Witwatersrand (range of mountains in south *Transvaal*, South *Africa*)
Afrikaans = 'white waters ridge'. Contains largest goldfield in the world,
so that familiar name of mountains, Rand, became word used as basic
unit of country's decimal currency in 1961.

Woomera (town in South *Australia*)
From aboriginal word = 'throwing stick' (not = English word 'boomer-
ang').

Worms (town in West *Germany* on River *Rhine,* north-west of *Mannheim*)
Ancient name was Borbetomagus, from personal name + Gaulish magos = 'field'. Name gradually shortened and changed (in 2nd century was Wormatia) to present form Worms.

Wrangel Island (in *Arctic* Ocean, off north-east coast of *Siberia,* USSR)
Named in 1867 in honour of Russian admiral and polar explorer Ferdinand von Wrangel (1796–1870) who led expedition in this region in 1820–4.

Wuppertal (city in west of West *Germany,* east of *Düsseldorf*)
From name of River Wupper, tributary of River *Rhine* (with name derived from wippeln = 'to hop along'), + German Tal = 'valley'. Name was given in 1929 to amalgamation of Barmen and Elberfeld with some smaller towns.

Württemberg (former kingdom in south-west of West *Germany*)
Now part of 'Land' of *Baden-Württemberg.* Originally was name of town, with 2nd element German Berg = 'mountain', and 1st element of uncertain origin—perhaps personal name or from Old High German root word = 'turn' (as in English 'vortex').

Wyoming (state in central west USA)
From Indian (Algonquian) meche-weami-ing = 'broad plains', originally applied to valley in east *Pennsylvania.* Name became popular through poem 'Gertrude of Wyoming' (1809) by Thomas Campbell and was officially adopted when state was formed in 1868.

Y **Yangtse-Kiang, River** (longest river in *Asia,* rising in central *China* and flowing mainly east into east China Sea near *Shanghai*)
Name derives from ancient city of Yangchow + Chinese kiang = 'river'. Chinese apply name only to lower reaches of river and call whole river Changkiang = 'long river'.

Yarra, River (in south *Victoria*, *Australia*, flowing west through *Melbourne* into *Port Phillip* Bay)
From aboriginal word = 'running water, river'.

Yellow River (2nd longest river in *China*, flowing mainly east and north into *Yellow Sea* south-west of *Peking*)
Name is English translation of Chinese name *Hwang-ho* (Huan-hei) = 'yellow river', referring to large quantities of silt (loess) it carries down.

Yellow Sea (inlet of *Pacific* between *Korea* and *China*)
Name is English translation of Chinese name Hwanghai = 'yellow sea', referring to dullish yellow colour of water caused by silt (loess) carried into it by *Yellow River*.

Yellowstone River (in *Wyoming* and *Montana*, USA)
Name is translation of earlier French name Roche Jaune = 'yellow rock', in turn probably translation of Indian nissi-a-dazi = 'river of yellow rocks'. River, tributary of *Missouri*, gave name to famous Yellowstone National Park.

Yemen (republic in south-west of Arabian peninsula, south of *Saudi Arabia*)
From Arabic = 'right', ie country lying on one's right hand as one faces *Mecca* (as opposed to Sham, territory in modern *Syria*, whose name = 'left').

Yenisei, River (in *Siberia*, USSR, flowing north into *Arctic* Ocean)
Name is Turkish variant, adopted by Russian population in 16th century, of native (Kanty, Selkup or Evenki) word iondessi = 'big river'.

Yerevan (capital of republic of *Armenia*, USSR)
Very old name, of uncertain meaning; perhaps = 'abode of the god Aru'. Not likely to be derived from name of founder (Khan Revan) or from Armenian yerevan = 'to appear' (in semi-jocular sense of 'first town to appear after the Flood').

Yokohama (4th largest city in *Japan*, seaport on *Honshu*, south of *Tokyo*)
From Japanese yoko = 'side' + kama = 'shore', ie 'cross shore'.

York, Cape (peninsula in north *Queensland, Australia*)
Name given in 1770 by Cook 'in honour of his late Royal Highness the Duke of York'.

Ypres (town in province of west *Flanders, Belgium*, south-west of *Ghent*)
From name of River Ypres (Flemish Ieper), with original form Ivara, of Celtic derivation with basic meaning = 'yew-tree'.

Yucatan (peninsula in Central *America* separating Gulf of *Mexico* from *Caribbean Sea*)
According to story, Spanish explorer Hernandez de Cordoba, landing here in 1517, asked Indian tribesmen what place was called and received reply 'tektetan' or 'yukatan' = 'I don't understand', which he took to be name of region. Or could be from Indian ki-u-tan = 'he speaks', tribal name, in sense of 'he who speaks our language'.

Yugoslavia (republic in south-east *Europe*)
From Slavonic yug = 'south' + Slavs, name of inhabitants, ie 'land of the southern Slavs'. Name of Slavs, as well as of Slovaks and Slovenes, derives possibly from Slavonic slava = 'fame' (ie 'famous people'), or from Slavonic slovo = 'word' (ie 'people who use the same words').

Yukon (territory in north-west *Canada*, bordering on *Alaska*)
Named after River Yukon, in turn with name from Indian word = 'big river'.

Z **Zagreb** (capital of *Croatia, Yugoslavia*, north-east of *Trieste*)
Recorded in 11th century but founded much earlier than this. Not likely to be from German Graben = 'trench, ditch', but from some Slavonic origin, perhaps = 'beyond the ditch (dam)'.

Zaire (republic in Central *Africa*)
From native name of River *Congo*, with African root za = 'river' (as in *Zambezi*). Until 1972 was Democratic Republic of *Congo*.

Zambezi, River (in *Africa*, rising in *Zambia* and flowing south-east into *Mozambique* Channel north-east of *Beira*)
From African word = 'big river' (African za = 'river'). Vasco da Gama, Portuguese explorer who first sighted its estuary in 1498 on his voyage to *India* named it Rio des Bons Sinães = 'river of good signs' (in sense that it showed him he was on correct course for *Asia*).

Zambia (republic in Central *Africa*)
From River *Zambezi*, which rises in north-west of republic. Until 1964 was Northern *Rhodesia*.

Zanzibar (island and its capital in Indian Ocean off coast of *Tanzania, Africa*)
From Arabic zang = 'black' + Iranian bar = 'coast, country', ie 'country of black-skinned people'. (Territory was under Arab rule in 8th–9th centuries.) Before 15th century name applied to East African coast here, not to island. In 1964 united with *Tanganyika* to form *Tanzania*.

Zeebrugge (seaport in *Belgium*, north of *Bruges*)
Town is port for *Bruges* (Flemish Brugge), so name = 'sea Bruges'. Two towns are linked by canal.

Zermatt (village and resort in *Switzerland* at foot of *Matterhorn*)
Name = 'on the meadow' (German zur Matte), and is related to *Matterhorn*.

Zuider Zee (former gulf of *North Sea*, north *Netherlands*)
Dutch = 'southern sea' (as opposed to *North Sea*). Today consists, after reclamation work begun 1920, of polders Waddenzee and Ijsselmeer.

Zürich (largest city in *Switzerland*)
Roman name was Turicum, from Celtic dur = 'water' + Latin suffix -icum; town is on shore of large lake which bears its name. Name changed to Zürich under influence of Germanic tribe Alemanni.

BIBLIOGRAPHICAL NOTE

The user of this book may wonder exactly where and how the various derivations were obtained. Authoritative toponymical works, if possible those with world-wide scope, are not plentiful, but three books—none of which is particularly easy to come by—were useful here: the German *Unsere Ortsnamen* (Our Place-Names) by W. Sturmfels and H. Bischof (Bonn, 1961), the Russian *Kratkiy toponimicheskiy slovar* (Concise Toponymical Dictionary) by V. A. Nikonov (Moscow, 1966) and the English *Names and Their Histories* (subtitled 'Handbook of Historical Geography and Topographical Nomenclature') by Isaac Taylor (London, 1896). The first two of these provide rich and reliable material on, respectively, Germanic and Slavonic names, and the last book, although published over three-quarters of a century ago, contains a wealth of detailed and fascinating information on names of truly world-wide range, and for its time is extraordinarily well documented. Canon Taylor must be regarded as a serious pioneer in the field of modern toponymy, and clearly carried out prolonged and scholarly researches before producing his book.

Turning to books dealing with a more specialised field, for English place-names throughout the world Mrs C. M. Matthews' *Place Names of the English-Speaking World* (London, 1972) is recommended, strongly supported by George R. Stewart's very comprehensive *American Place Names* (New York, 1970) and G. H. Armstrong's *The Origin and Meaning of Place Names in Canada* (Toronto, 1930). I have also used *The New Zealand Guide* by E. S. Dollimore (Dunedin, 1962) and H. G. R. King's interesting book *The Antarctic* (London, 1969).

For additional information on French names—important if one is studying French as a first foreign language—I found the *Dictionnaire étymologique des noms de lieux en France* by A. Dauzat and C. Rostaing (Paris, 1963) helpful, although it deals only with inhabited places (towns, villages and the like) and not, for example, with mountains or rivers.

Naturally, a good deal of checking of facts and figures had to be done—especially where two or more books gave different data—and for this I turned chiefly to two works: *Everyman's Dictionary of Dates*, edited by Audrey Butler (London, 1971), and W. G. Moore's *The Penguin Encyclo-*

pedia of Places (London, 1971). The latter book proved invaluable for establishing the geographical location of places, and frequently provided useful historical background information.

For cross-checking recent changes of name I found Hebe Spaull's little book *New Place Names of the World* (London, 1970) of assistance, although 'kingdoms rise and wane' with such increasing rapidity that a constant eye has had to be kept on the daily press in order to be as up-to-date as possible with current renamings.

It goes without saying that such books as these are not enough. Some names are difficult to track down. A reliable encyclopedia, such as the *Encyclopaedia Britannica*, can help, or sometimes a book which, while not claiming to deal primarily with place-name derivations, can still furnish an explanation, or at least give a clue: such books range from historical and geographical works to travel guides and tourist brochures. Quite frequently an all-round reference work such as a dictionary or *Payton's Proper Names* are helpful, and so too were the special reports on individual countries published periodically by *The Times*. (For the very great and valuable help I received from individuals and official bodies, I offer separate Acknowledgements.)

For the checking of the meanings of foreign words recourse foreign-language dictionaries are of course essential, although for the meanings of words in ancient or extinct languages such as Sanskrit or Gaulish I have relied almost exclusively on the toponymists themselves. I am aware of the dangers of this, as they in turn have in many cases obtained their linguistic derivations from other sources, and—like place-names themselves—errors and corruptions and miscopyings can creep in when words are transcribed by one writer from another. For *my* miscopyings—which I hope are few—I am alone to blame, but for the mistranscriptions of others I would prefer not to be held responsible!

Last, but obviously by no means least, I have at all stages tried to get as close as possible to the place and its name without actually going there. For in the first place compiling a 'short list' of names for inclusion I used *The Penguin Encyclopedia of Places*, *Whitaker's Almanack*, the *Post Office Guide* and the wall map of the world published by the *Daily Express* (London, 1972). For more detailed 'map-work', and especially for spellings, I constantly referred to two atlases: *Philips' Record Atlas* (London, 1965) and *Philips' Concorde World Atlas* (London, 1972).

ACKNOWLEDGEMENTS

I could not possibly have completed this book without the assistance of a number of people, many of whom either put me on to or loaned me invaluable source material, or who answered, frequently exhaustively and most interestingly, specific queries that I had put to them.

I am particularly grateful to Mr Leslie Dunkling, President of the Names Society, who right from the conception of the book has advised me about useful source books and has also kindly obtained for me or loaned me books that have helped considerably in my work.

I should also like to express my indebtedness to the following, who have not only supplied interesting and valuable copies of original material but who have furnished most useful toponymical bibliographies: Mr W. T. Cations of the National Library of Australia in London; Mrs Elizabeth R. Ziman of the United States Library, London University; Mrs Eleanor Martin of the Canadian High Commission in London, and Miss S. Fryer of the New Zealand High Commission in London.

For answering most fully individual queries that I had put to them I wish also to thank the following, who in a number of cases supplemented their information with helpful supporting material: Monsieur J. Lefillatre, Administrateur en Chef, St Pierre et Miquelon; Mr J. D. Murray, CMG, HM Chargé d'Affaires and Consul, Haiti; Mr Raymond Falle of the States of Jersey Library Service; Mrs P. N. Frost of the Consulate General of Monaco, London; Monsieur Pierre Steinmetz, Directeur de Cabinet, High Commission of New Caledonia; Mr E. W. Namatika of the Malawi High Commission, London, and the Librarian of the Institut Français du Royaume-Uni, London.

To all these, and to others whom I have not individually acknowledged here, I wish to offer my thanks and express my gratitude for their practical advice, information and encouragement. To tackle such a wealth of material single-handed has not been easy, and many friends have helped in what at times has seemed an almost impossible task: that of compressing into a limited compass a representative selection of the world's better-known place-names.